MEG ANNE BRIGHTON

The Girl with the Golden Ribbon

The Brier Hill Series Book One

First published by Nora Bross- Owner of Lindsey Barker Books 2021

Copyright © 2021 by Meg Anne Brighton

All rights reserved. No part of this publication may be reproduced, stored or transmitted in any form or by any means, electronic, mechanical, photocopying, recording, scanning, or otherwise without written permission from the publisher. It is illegal to copy this book, post it to a website, or distribute it by any other means without permission.

This novel is entirely a work of fiction. The names, characters and incidents portrayed in it are the work of the author's imagination. Any resemblance to actual persons, living or dead, events or localities is entirely coincidental.

Meg Anne Brighton asserts the moral right to be identified as the author of this work.

Meg Anne Brighton has no responsibility for the persistence or accuracy of URLs for external or third-party Internet Websites referred to in this publication and does not guarantee that any content on such Websites is, or will remain, accurate or appropriate.

Designations used by companies to distinguish their products are often claimed as trademarks. All brand names and product names used in this book and on its cover are trade names, service marks, trademarks and registered trademarks of their respective owners. The publishers and the book are not associated with any product or vendor mentioned in this book. None of the companies referenced within the book have endorsed the book.

Book cover designed by Meg Anne Brighton. Font by Jessica Allain.

Second edition

ISBN: 9780997381900

This book was professionally typeset on Reedsy.
Find out more at reedsy.com

To my children and grandchildren,

Jeffrey, Michael, and Christina
Michael Joseph, Joey, Kiley Josephine
Nick and Christian
Ella and Chloe

With Love Forever

Fairy tales are more than true; not because they tell us that dragons exist, but because they tell us that dragons can be beaten.

G.K. Chesterton

Contents

Acknowledgments	iii
A Date	1
Thomas Shrock	9
The Black Dress	19
Fireflies	24
First Kiss	34
Mistletoe	40
Revenge	46
Floozy	52
Ludwig Castle	60
The Dark Tower	62
Damien	69
Lillian Warns of Grave Dangers	78
Snitch	81
Leaving Ludwig Castle	90
The Phantom Horseman	93
Sawyer Rhodes	98
The Exorcism	101
Maverick Lover	110
The Storm Within	115
The Sorceress	120
The Golden Goose	124
Rather Kiss a Rattlesnake	130
The Last Seal	138
Amulets and Charms	144
Black Ribbons	150

Gargoyles and Tombstones	154
The Rolltop Desk	158
Secrets in Nell Rhodes Closet	162
Guilt Ridden	169
The Note	175
The Confession	182
The Sorceress and The Seven Witches	186
The Wizard and Damien	190
The Masquerade	194
The Crimson Bedchamber	198
Home, At Last	204
Bella Franz	207
The Log Cabin	211
A Rooster Crowed Twice	218
The Wedding	226
The Celebration	231
About the Author	234
Also by Meg Anne Brighton	235

Acknowledgments

A huge thank you to my editor, Loretta Leslie, who has been an incredible source of support and encouragement throughout this journey, as well as a friend.

A special thank you to my family, whose love and support have meant the world to me.

A Date

The fireplace was roaring in the study, and Judge Daniel Stratford sat in a well-worn leather chair, smoking his pipe. His daughter, Stephanie, curled up in an overstuffed chair and covered her legs with a white throw. Her mother's Persian cat, Simone, jumped onto her lap. She stroked the cat's head, and a loud purring filled the room.

"The Christmas party at the Country Club is coming up next Saturday night, and Richard Cooper would like you to be his date," Daniel said. "What do you think?"

"A date?" Stephanie said, eyeing him with suspicion. He had talked about Richard Cooper at length at dinner, full of praise for Richard's thriving law practice and the old mansion he had turned into his law office. It had impressed Marguerite that the mansion, built in the 1800s, was on the National Register of Historic Places.

Stephanie's cheeks burned. "He's older, Daddy, and I doubt we'd have anything in common." Her father looked tired; she hoped he would believe the color in her cheeks was from the roaring fire. His dark hair had turned grayer, and his shoulders slumped a little. She fixed her gaze on him, knowing she would not win.

"Honey, you're too hard on yourself. You're beautiful, intelligent, and you traveled all over the world with Hedy. You and Richard have everything in common."

"That's sweet of you to say, Daddy, but a man like Richard is used to glamorous women. He has a bit of a reputation for being a ladies' man."

"That was years ago, when he was a football hero. In case you haven't heard, he's now a lawyer, and his practice is going well. I had lunch with him and Parker the other day, and he asked about you. He was wondering if you already have a date for the dance. When I told him you were going with us as usual, he suggested you go as a couple."

"I didn't realize Richard had come home. The last time I saw him was at the Country Club dance when I was sixteen. He had a date, but he asked me to dance, and I was so embarrassed because I was wearing this frilly dress like the one Scarlett O'Hara wore in *Gone with the Wind*. Marguerite bought it in Charleston. I thought I would die when he asked me to dance. So, we're dancing, and he told me I was stunning and that he'd been admiring me all evening. I was blushing and praying he wouldn't remember that the last time we were together at a family event—I bit him because he wouldn't let me win at chess."

"How old were you, Steph?"

"That's the problem. I was 12, and he was 19."

"I wouldn't worry about it—I doubt he remembers."

"You don't understand, Daddy. I drew blood."

"He said something else that I've never forgotten—he whispered in my ear and said that one day we would have an actual date together and that he would never forget this dance and the way I looked. When the dance was over, he told me to look him straight in the eye because he was going to take a picture of me in his mind and hold it in his heart until I met him again."

"Sounds like Richard was smitten with you—even then."

"That's not all," Stephanie said. "After he gazed at me, he told me to shut my eyes. Then I felt his lips brush mine, and he told me that was my sweet sixteen kiss."

Daniel's eyes danced as he reminisced. "Hard to believe it's been four years. That night was like a 'coming out' for you, and Marguerite wanted to show you off."

"I'm well aware. She pinched my cheeks all evening because she didn't want me to wear make-up, and she plastered my lips with lip gloss." With belligerence in her tone, she said, "I will never wear another dress that Marguerite picks out. Hedy shopped in Paris, the fashion mecca of the world. I would be happy with any dress she owned. She knew about style, Daddy."

"Hedy kept up on the latest fashion, but there's something about seeing you in my dead mother's clothes that freaks me out. Besides, a natural beauty like you shouldn't compare yourself to other women."

"You're only saying that because you're my father. Thinking about going on a date with Richard makes me jittery. He could have any girl he wanted. If I go — I have to do something with myself — I have to look amazing."

"Richard will like whatever you wear," he said, getting up from his easy chair and throwing another log on the fire. He poured himself another whiskey from the decanter, and the ice cubes clinked together when he put them in his crystal glass. "Your nightcap," he said as he handed her an apéritif of sherry in a crystal glass.

Stephanie sipped the sherry, feeling the hotness in her throat. "What's wrong, Daddy?" she asked. Her father was staring into the fireplace at the flames, deep in thought.

"It's bittersweet watching you grow up," he said, putting his feet up on the ottoman. "I know it's been hard for you with Hedy gone. Marguerite has never been much of a mother. She's always been a social butterfly. And I depended on Hedy and Emily to give you the maternal nourishment and love you needed."

"My grandmother meant the world to me. I have so many wonderful memories. We did everything together; she taught me how to cook and entertain. I traveled the world with her. She sent me to a cooking school in Europe, where we shopped and visited art galleries. I feel very well equipped to be on my own." She paused. "My nanny, Emily, taught me how to sew and keep my room neat and organized, and there's so much more." She could never name everything the two women had taught her throughout the years.

Daniel stared into his goblet. "But you know nothing about men. My mother created a fairytale world and told you that you would marry a handsome prince one day." He chuckled, "You read every fairy tale you could get your hands on."

"Fairy tales were my favorite books when I was little, and I still love the Walt Disney movies, especially *Beauty and the Beast.*" She paused. "You are the best example of what a husband and father should be, and I know I'll find no one like you. It would be impossible. So, I will be like Jane Austin, write books and never marry. I love Brighton House with you and Marguerite so close by. It's an idyllic life."

He stared into the fire as if he were searching for answers. "What you don't understand, Stephanie, is that life changes. You need to bring more people into your life. Marguerite and I won't be around forever. It's my responsibility to guide you through life, especially now that Hedy is gone. You're grown up now and never dated, and I'm sensing that you're floundering. I'm not good at this sort of thing, but let's go shopping tomorrow and buy you a new gown for the Christmas dance and some nice clothes. We'll have a father-daughter day."

"What about Marguerite?"

"She's working on another charity."

Stephanie looked pensive. "You worry too much, Daddy. A lot of guys at college have asked me out, but I'd rather do other things. It's a choice. I don't need a man to validate who I am, but I'll go to the party with Richard if it makes you happy."

He didn't know she had a clandestine romance with her nanny's son, Thomas Shrock, since she was fifteen. It had started as a crush, but a romance between an Amish girl and an English boy was against every rule in the county, and she didn't dare tell her parents. After starting college, they had drifted apart.

Stephanie yawned. "Night, Daddy. I'll see you tomorrow."

"Almost forgot to tell you—I asked Thomas Shrock to come by tomorrow morning and take you to cut your Christmas tree."

Her mouth gaped. "Thomas Shrock? You should have said something, Daddy. I'm still unpacking, and in the afternoon we're going shopping."

"He knows where the best trees are," Daniel said. "I'm lucky Thomas could do it. I hear his cabinet business is thriving. He's a rich man now and has bought more land. The Amish are smart—when they buy up as much land as they can. Now that you've inherited Brighton House, you are the most prominent landowner in the county."

"So they tell me," Stephanie said in a bored tone. "Mother says I'm filthy rich, but I wouldn't know anything about that because you keep me on a strict allowance. I've been meaning to talk to you about increasing it. After all, I'm twenty, and I've been responsible, haven't I?"

"You're responsible, but you have a lot to learn, especially about investments."

"I'll do it this summer," Stephanie said. "Right now, I have to get ready for Christmas and decorate Brighton House. The house means everything to me—that's where all my memories of Hedy are, and I feel like the luckiest girl in the world that she left it to me."

Daniel grinned. "I believe you're right, Stephanie. You are the luckiest girl in the world."

There was a full moon, and Stephanie enjoyed the brisk walk. Her little dog, Brooks, ran ahead of her, sniffing. When she heard a rustle, she paid little attention, but when a horned owl swooped down so close that she could feel the wind from its wings, she cried out. She broke into a run—her heart pounding.

It was only Owl, but he had scared her. She felt foolish. It used to be fun when she was young, but she no longer had time for such things. When she was twelve, her father asked her not to talk to the owl anymore because it wasn't normal. Owl's feathers ruffled when she told him, and she swore she saw tears well up in huge yellow eyes.

"Okay, we'll still talk, but not as much, and never around father." Owl never left her and flew behind her car when she went off to college. He was protective and followed her back to the dormitory when she studied late at the library. Stephanie could feel his huge eyes on her as she jogged down the path covered with a blanket of snow.

"It's cold, Owl. You must go to the barn to sleep tonight," she said, looking up and meeting his gaze. When she went up to her bedroom, she peered out her window to see if he was still in the tree. In the moonlight, she could see him spread his wings and fly away, heading toward the barn.

Stephanie both felt tired and excited when she went to bed. The flannel nightgown felt warm and cozy. Boots curled up beside her, and Brooks lay at her feet. The thought of going shopping with her father lifted her spirits. Before turning out the light, she'd picked up the black book from her nightstand, eager to read more about the cursed babe. She'd found the desk last night, locked away in her grandmother's old vintage desk.

Stephanie turned the pages in rapt anticipation as she read the book.

Joseph's eyes clouded as he watched them drive away. He was pinning his hopes on strangers. They would love her, but could they keep her safe? He felt a pang of guilt that he had not dared tell them that the wizard had already been there to claim her. When they read the black book, they would discover the truth for themselves. Then they would understand that the Feathered Pen was magic. She would never have a secret. The Feathered Pen would reveal everything she did.

Though his heart was heavy, there was no time to mourn. He prayed to God Almighty and all the angels and saints for an intervention, but it didn't come. He knew then what he must do, as much as it filled him with dread. It was his only hope.

Later that night, Joseph lifted the mysterious key from the nightstand. He paused at his door to scan the corridor to ensure that he was alone. What he was about to do would cause expulsion from the monastery. At the foot of the stairs to the tower where the locked room was, he paused. He needed to summon his courage for what was to come. Each step he took eroded his will, but he had to see this through for the child's sake. He inserted the key in the lock. There was no turning back now. The door creaked on rusted hinges, and he glanced down the stairs, fearing someone would hear. On a stand in a corner was a dusty, ancient book that looked as if it hadn't been opened in eons. He remembered the thrill he had experienced when he had explored its mysteries. How had something this powerful made its way into the monastery? Now he would say the magic words that he had discovered. Joseph pulled back the rug. Underneath, a circle and a star were embedded in the marble floor. He had learned that this was a place of protection, and as he stood in the middle chanting the words, his nerves were tingling. Would it work? It had worked before. He started when the apparition appeared framed in fire. It was a shock to his senses. He had done it. He had summoned Lucifer.

Lucifer's dark eyes flashed. "Are we in agreement?"

"Yes, I will give up my face to you if you will break the Wizard's curse," Joseph said.

"You are a handsome man," Lucifer replied. "It is a heavy price to pay."

"It is a small price to pay to save my daughter from a marriage to an evil prince," Joseph said. "He is the darkest prince in all the kingdoms."

"Your daughter was born perfect. She will be the most beautiful woman in all the kingdoms. To save her from her fate, I may need something more to break the curse. The Wizard is mighty."

Joseph's expression was sorrowful. "I have no money or possessions. I took the vow of poverty."

"We will settle up later." Lucifer's hand touched Joseph's handsome face, and it disappeared in a heavy mist. Two enormous eyes peered out, roving about in a black space in his brown hooded robe.

"Henceforth, you shall be called Ochre Eyes, the monk who delves in the dark," Lucifer declared. "Your work on earth is done. You will go with me to Ludwig Castle. I will give you powers."

As sleep overtook her, she fell into a dream state, and the black book dropped from her hand.

The monk, Ochre Eyes, appeared at her bedside. His huge yellow eyes gazed upon her with a look of adoration.

She stirred when his hand reached out and brushed her cheek.

"Daughter," he whispered before fading away into the darkness.

She slept, the moonlight streaming through the white curtains on her lovely face.

Thomas Shrock

Stephanie roused, the light streaming in the bedroom window, casting a soft yellow glow. She sighed and snuggled into the covers, relieved it had only been a dream. She frowned at the black book lying beside her on the pillow.

"Enough of you," she said, tossing the book aside. "You gave me a nightmare—the worst I've ever had."

Stephanie bounced out of bed, eager for the day to begin. Thomas Shrock was coming this morning, and they would go to the forest and cut the Christmas tree.

Thomas was right on time. When she answered the door, her cheeks flushed with embarrassment. He had been her crush before she left for college. After that, their relationship had slowly disintegrated.

He stood, looking at her with a question in his gray eyes, dressed all in black, and she thought his clothes looked new. An Amish man's dress was usually the same, but there was something different. Maybe it was the money. Her father had said his cabinet business, Fritz and Thomas, was thriving, and he was a rich man. He looked like Ryan Gosling and appeared taller and more self-confident than she remembered, but he still had a bit of a boyish look.

"Good morning," she said with a slight smile, unsure of where she stood with him.

Thomas raised his brows, but didn't speak as he loomed over Stephanie, tall and lanky. Three years older, he had been her crush since the age of fifteen. Her heart skipped a beat as her feelings for him resurfaced. There was a chill, and it wasn't just the weather. The silence as they walked to the buckboard stung her conscience further.

"Hello, Maybell," Stephanie said, reaching up and rubbing one of the two large Percheron horses behind the ears while she gathered her thoughts.

Maybell nickered.

"At least someone is glad to see me," she said under her breath, feeling nervous, not knowing where she stood with Thomas. Her jaw clenched when she thought about the rumors she'd heard about Thomas being with Maddie Yoder, an Amish girl who went to his church.

Thomas helped her into the wagon, then reached into the back and gave her a black wool throw. The action was comforting, but his silence was not. The ride was bumpy, and when they turned down a narrow lane towards the field, it threw her against his lanky frame. She caught her breath, and when their eyes met in a veil of white vapor, she could see the anguish in his face.

"How are you?" he asked, casting a glance at her, his tone as icy as the tree branches.

"Busy with school, and trying to keep up with Brighton House. I moved out of the dormitory because of the constant noise, which made it challenging to keep up with my grades. I'm living in a boarding house owned by an old family friend, Clare Grant. She used to visit my grandmother, and they would have tea in the garden. She's helped me so much with Hedy's death. Her nephew is my history professor."

His gray eyes examined her with scrutiny. "What happened to the girl I used to know? Have you given me or my family a second thought since you started college? It isn't just me—you were best friends with my sister, Mary. Mother suffers the most—you were like a daughter to her. She and your grandmother raised you from an infant. You were part of our family."

"It was difficult for me, too. I had to choose my path, Thomas. I felt torn. You know, Daddy would go ballistic if he knew about us."

Thomas gazed at her. "I wish we'd done more. By now, we could have been married with children."

Stephanie dropped her eyes, hesitant to tell him it wasn't the life she wanted. She'd made her choice and didn't want a domestic life. She loved her freedom and wanted to travel the world and become a famous author.

The only sounds were the horses clomping through the deep snow as they followed the white fencing along a path that led to a field of pines in the distance.

Stephanie reached out and touched his arm. "What about you, Thomas? There was a rumor you were dating Maddie Yoder. I thought you'd be married by now."

He flinched.

"How can I marry Maddie when I'm in love with you?"

Stephanie looked pained. "We can never be together, Thomas. Our cultural differences won't allow it. I'm Catholic and you're Amish, and nothing will ever change that. Anyway, it doesn't matter. We've both changed since I started college."

"It's a lame excuse," Thomas said with a crease between his brow. He sighed. "You're like the changing seasons—I liked you better in the summer. You were sweeter—college has changed you. Remember two years ago at Rumspringa—what it was like lying on the blanket with the moon and the stars? I was as poor as a church mouse, and you were eighteen and hadn't started college yet. I would give anything to go back to that day and do it all over again."

Stephanie smiled, remembering. She could tell by his tone that he had softened. She ventured to slip her arm in his and snuggled close, loving the warmth of his body. When they approached the pines, she looked up at the massive snow-flocked spruce and asked, "What about that one?"

"You have a tall ceiling, but not that tall." He laughed, and it gladdened her heart. "I marked a tree in the spring that will suit, and I know exactly where it is."

"Why, Thomas Schrock! You didn't tell me."

"Haw," he commanded, flicking the reins. Shortly, he pulled up to a perfectly shaped spruce pine.

She felt serene, surrounded by the beauty of the tall pines and a blanket of snow. Thomas helped her down from the buckboard. In the stillness, as he held her close, she slid against him, her feet not touching the ground. It hit her with a ton of emotions when she realized Thomas was holding her tightly and gazing into her eyes. A deep feeling of intimacy consumed her—just like she'd felt when she was fifteen. At age fifteen, sparks had flown between them when he'd helped her off her horse. They didn't act on it, but the attraction had started there. At that moment, she thought she would die if he didn't kiss her.

"If you're wondering if I remember that day when you were fifteen—I do." A shadow of pain crossed Thomas's face.

"You can still read my mind, Thomas," she said.

She heard her boots crunch into the snow. His arms dropped from around her. She watched him turn and walk away. The day would have been so perfect if he had kissed me. Her face grew hot.

"What's holding you back now, Thomas? Are you still afraid of my father, or is it because of Maddie?"

"Neither." He pulled a long-handled ax out of the wagon, then shed his jacket. "You're a rich girl now, and all you think about is books. What would you want with me?"

"There's nothing wrong with kissing, Thomas. The girls at college kiss guys all the time—different ones every night."

Thomas raised his brow. "Do they? What about you—did you meet someone?"

"Why do you care?" Stephanie asked.

He set his jaw. "Let's get the work done."

Stephanie could see his muscles through the black, long-sleeved shirt he was wearing. She watched, amazed by his strength as the ax thudded against the tree. He had felled the tall tree with three swings. Then he picked it up by its heavy branches and heaved it onto the wagon.

On the way home, the horse needed encouragement to pull the heavy tree. Thomas gave commands to the horse but said nothing to her.

Out of sheer frustration, she said, "What's wrong?"

"Can't you see that the tree is large, and it's a heavy load in the snow for the horses?"

"It isn't just the horses that are stressed," she said. "Why can't we talk about it? I still care about you, Thomas. It's just that..."

"We've grown apart," he said. "I wasn't enough."

"It wasn't you, Thomas. You were more than enough."

His jaw twitched. "If that were true, we would be married. Instead, you're a college student, and I'm a deacon."

"A deacon?" she asked, surprised.

"Yes. I now help the bishop, and sometimes we hold church services in my new barn. We had a barn raising, and it's the most enormous barn in the county."

She'd lost touch and was tense with nervous energy. Arriving at Brighton House was a relief. Despite her pent-up feelings, she took a moment to admire the Victorian-style country estate and was determined to decorate it in the same style as Hedy. She reminded herself to put red bows on the fence posts of the white fencing.

"I'll help you carry in the tree," she said, hoping the offer would please him.

He jumped down and wrapped the reins around the hitching post. "I'd rather you make hot chocolate."

Thomas helped her down from the wagon, holding her at arm's length.

Disappointment crept into her face, but she didn't want to antagonize him further.

"Don't look," Thomas said. "But Becca is peeking out from the curtains in the upstairs window. Mother says she eavesdrops and tells your father everything. Send her home early if you can."

Stephanie looked up at the window. Becca stepped back and dropped the curtain. There wasn't a lot she could do about the forty-two-year-old spinster who was not likely to change. She had come with the house and would always be a fixture. It was her grandmother's wish in her will that Becca remain on as the housekeeper. Stephanie adhered to her grandmother's wishes even though Becca read her mail, drank the whiskey that was for guests and her father's visits, and had never kept a secret. She was like a magpie, collecting bits and pieces of information, but never repeating a story the same way twice.

Stephanie thought Thomas looked handsome as his tall, black-clad frame leaned into the doorway. She was aware of his eyes on her as he sipped a cup of hot chocolate. She fiddled with her hair and pushed it behind her ear as she rummaged through a box of decorations.

"Nice shirt," she said, a smile curving at her lips. "Is it new?" He was frugal, but she'd heard that his cabinet business in Brier Hill was growing by leaps and bounds. The Amish were modest and hid their wealth. She knew Thomas wouldn't say anything unless she prodded him.

"Yah, I bought myself a few new things." His gray eyes settled on her ears. "Do you need a new scarf? Your ears are red—you had nothing on your head."

She went up two rungs on the ladder. "I couldn't find my scarf this morning." She began placing Victorian decorations on the Christmas tree.

"What girl who lives in this kind of weather can't find their scarf?" He spoke with an intensity that chilled the air. "Did you lose my phone number, too?"

Stephanie looked up, surprised. She'd never heard him show so much emotion. His expression told her he was waiting for a reaction. She sighed as if she had the world on her shoulders. "Thomas, you don't understand."

His brows creased. "I haven't heard from you for months, and I deserve an explanation. Had your father not called and asked me to cut the tree and chop firewood, I wouldn't have known you were home from college."

She bit her lip. "I needed more, Thomas. Daddy said it was my time to shine, and that's what I did. It doesn't mean I don't care for you because I do. It's just that you're all about religion, Thomas—marriage and babies. It's not what I want."

"What do you want?"

"This is what I want—Brighton House, and my books, an education, and interesting people to spend time with. I have everything I want, Thomas, but it hasn't been easy."

The six-bedroom, sprawling house was a lot of responsibility. She'd cleaned out closets and drawers, sent fifteen boxes to the thrift shop, and winterized the house before she left for college. Thomas's mother, Emily, had a going-away dinner for her, but his entire family was there, and they had not been alone. Keeping up her grades at college had been difficult. She was finding it increasingly difficult to balance her life. There was never enough time. And now that she was back, she had to get ready for Christmas. Her shoulders slumped. Even though she had explained, she knew Thomas would not let it go.

She breathed a sigh of relief when Becca appeared, holding a tattered angel that Hedy always put on top of the tree. "I dusted her off. She was in a box separate from the other decorations. I almost didn't see her."

Stephanie moved higher up the ladder, and Thomas stood at the bottom to steady it. She hesitated when Becca handed her the angel. "Oh dear, she goes on top of the tree, and I can't reach. Thomas, would you mind?"

In an instant, he had grabbed her around her tiny waist, lifting her down from the ladder. It was sudden, and his nearness set her heart aflutter, but she hid her emotions and murmured. "Thomas, you should have warned me. I might have dropped her." She handed him the tattered angel. "She's over a hundred years old, but she's still beautiful."

Thomas' agile body scaled the ladder in an instant, and he placed the angel on the treetop. "How's that, Steph?"

"Perfect," she said with a satisfied smile. "She's tattered, but it doesn't show because she's on top, and the tree is so tall." But the angel didn't hold and tumbled down the tree, grazing over the branches, coming to rest at Stephanie's feet. The angel's blue eyes stared up at her as if they held a secret.

"I hope she's not broken," Stephanie said, reaching down for her.

"It's a sign," Becca said in a mysterious voice. "Someone will fall from grace. That's what Hedy always said happens when an angel falls from the tree."

Stephanie brushed off the angel. "It's an old wives' tale. Try again, Thomas," she said, holding the angel up to him. When their fingers touched, a shiver went through her. Something seemed off-kilter.

"Look," Becca said, holding a tiny sliver of porcelain from the doll on her finger.

"It's nothing," Stephanie said. "Put it in an envelope and put it on my desk. I'll glue it back on when we take down the tree next year."

Thomas shot her a pained look—a reminder she needed to send Becca home early.

"Take the rest of the day off, Becca. Thomas and I can finish the tree. I'm sure you have plenty to do at home."

"If you don't need me, I'll go," Becca said. "But I'll make up my time."

"Oh, no. I won't hear of it. Grab some Christmas cookies on the way out. Marguerite made them. They're delicious."

"That was slick," Thomas said when Becca was out of earshot.

Stephanie grinned. "Hedy taught me a thing or two, but I learned how to dismiss people from Marguerite. She always told me it's not what you say, but how you say it."

"Will you dismiss me that way, too? Grab some cookies on the way out the door, Thomas."

"Don't mock me," she scolded. But then she laughed. Thomas seemed to be in a better mood. When she stood back to admire the angel, she also took in Thomas's lean, well-proportioned body. He was sexy, and she thought he knew it. It wasn't any secret that Thomas was the most eligible Amish bachelor in the county. He had all the traits that she admired in a man: gentle, peace-loving, a sexy charisma, and a laid-back attitude that drew her to him.

She knew from Thomas's sister, Mary, that several girls at church had their eye on him. The most persistent person was Maddie Yoder.

She threw her arms around his waist when he came down the ladder.

"I missed you," she said, putting her head against his strong back, her hands clasped around his waist.

"Did you?" he said. "After not hearing from you for months, you're home, and you want to pick up where we left off when you haven't even said you're sorry."

When he pulled her hands apart and turned around, she wished he hadn't because his gray eyes were reproachful.

"I'm so sorry," she said. "Not that I want to pick up where we left off—I just want to be friends. And maybe even more than friends." She bit her lip. He was a pious man—how could she tell him what was on her mind? She found him attractive, but she didn't want to marry him. Like the other girls at college, Stephanie was ready to explore her sexuality without commitment. *Isn't that what Jane Austen had done?*

"My entire family was worried."

Stephanie knew from the pain in his voice that he was losing his self-restraint.

Bitterness hung in his words. "No one heard a word from you, not even Mary."

"You've always been my rock, especially after Hedy died. I'll make it all up to you." She paused. She'd always shared her deepest feelings with Thomas, but she wasn't sure he'd understand. "Last night, I saw Hedy sitting in the chair in the library."

Thomas's brows creased. It wasn't the Amish way to mourn for lengthy periods, and Stephanie knew that the mention of Hedy had rankled him. He cupped her chin, but his words belied the gentle action. "Your mind is playing tricks on you. Hedy is dead, and she can't come back."

"It's hard not to think about her when I'm living in her house."

"You've had plenty of time to mourn. I didn't come here today to talk about Hedy. I want to talk about 'us.' When in God's name are you going to let Hedy rest in peace?"

"Thomas, I thought you, of all people, would understand. You're the only one I can talk to—please try to understand." She trembled. "There's more. I found a black book in Hedy's desk in a secret compartment…"

Thomas could not hide his look of surprise. "You did not open the book, did you, Stephanie?" His worried gray eyes bore into hers. "Tell me you did not open the book."

Stephanie drew back, flummoxed. "I opened it and I've been reading it."

Thomas grabbed her by the shoulders. "This is one book you must not read, Stephanie. Please give it to me. I must take it to the bishop."

"So, you know about the book?"

"Yes. My mother locked the book away in the secret compartment of Hedy's desk."

"How do you know about it?"

"Mother told me about it four years ago, after she found out I'd carved our initials on the oak tree in the woods. Mary couldn't keep our secret."

Stephanie drew in a sharp breath. "I didn't know Emily knew about us."

"Mother was afraid that Judge might find out about us, but she also thought I should know about the black book. She said that you were an infant, and Hedy was looking for a place to hide the book. My father made the secret compartment in the desk, and it was never to be opened. Hedy always kept the desk locked."

"I don't understand," Stephanie said, flummoxed. "The key to the desk was on a chest in my bedroom."

"The day Hedy died, she gave the key to my mother. It was in our house." Thomas's voice was forceful. "You must give me the book. I'll take it to the bishop."

"I'm sorry, Thomas, but I cannot give it up. At least not yet. I have to find out what happens to the girl."

Thomas's complexion paled. "The black book has bewitched you, Stephanie. Do you understand what I'm saying? You must give it to me before it's too late."

"No," Stephanie said, jutting her chin. "You're being unreasonable. It's only a dark fairy tale. We'll talk about it later. I have to get ready to go to dinner with my father."

"Call me when you get home," he said with a sense of urgency. "I'll be waiting…like I've been waiting for months."

The Black Dress

Stephanie found the perfect dress when she and her father went shopping. It was black and split up the leg.

"It's elegant and sophisticated. You have the legs for this dress," the saleslady said. "You can't go wrong in black. And it shows just enough cleavage to make it interesting."

When Stephanie put her hands on her hips and struck a pose in front of her father, waiting for his approval, she detected a tear in his eye.

"You've grown up right before my eyes," he said with a choked voice. There was silence, and then his expression changed to a broad smile. "Richard will love it."

They had a steak dinner at an upscale Cameron Mitchell restaurant. After dinner, they had an espresso coffee, and Daniel reflected on her childhood. "One of my fondest memories is coming home for work and finding you waiting for me. You would stand on my shoes, and we would dance."

Stephanie smiled and nodded. "I remember watching out the window for you to come home. It was my favorite time of day."

"Mine, too," he said, looking into his coffee cup, avoiding her eyes as he fought his emotions. "Don't stand on Richard's feet when you dance, Steph."

She laughed, and his eyes twinkled. It was almost as if he had a secret and was withholding something from her. She let it go, thinking he was having difficulty watching her grow up.

It was after nine o'clock when Stephanie got home, and she was glad Becca had left the outside lights on. She changed into her slippers in the mudroom and put the teapot on. Then she padded into the drawing room and lit the Christmas tree. When she turned around, an enormous vase of red roses sitting on the piano caught her off balance. Her first thought was that the deliveryman had made a mistake. Marguerite always ordered a lot of flowers during the Christmas season. She was sure they were Marguerite's.

When she read the card, she thought her heart would leap right out of her chest.

Can't wait to see you. Love Richard.

Overflowing with happiness, Stephanie sat down in an overstuffed chair, rereading the card. She'd never received flowers from anyone except family members for special occasions, and never anything like this. She counted them; there were twenty-four perfect, unblemished red roses. After she composed herself, she went to the kitchen and made herself a cup of tea. The teapot was whistling, and she couldn't help but smile as she poured the tea, thrilled about the card.

The world seemed brighter as she carried her packages up to her room and hung up the new pants she'd bought. New clothes always lifted her mood, and she reflected on the excellent day she'd had with her father as she put away the sweaters, black heels, and makeup she had purchased. That's when she noticed the black book on the floor, open to a picture of the dark prince. She thought the book must have fallen when she made the bed this morning.

Stephanie gazed at his face, mesmerized. There was no doubt about it—he was a handsome devil. "Hello, handsome," she murmured, her eyes scrutinizing his face, noticing every detail. The prince's dark eyes glinted in the light, holding a promise of danger. His chiseled jawline and determined expression revealed a hint of ruthlessness.

There was a loud thud against the window, and she jumped in surprise. She strained her ears but could only hear the faint sound of the wind. She gazed at the prince's face one more time, and something seemed different. There was a slight curve to his lips, as if he were smiling, but she knew the prince had not been smiling a moment ago.

"No, no," she said with fear in her voice, "this cannot be happening." She heeded Thomas's warning and slammed the book shut as a surge of panic rose in her chest.

To take her mind off the picture, she checked her Christmas card list to make sure it was correct. Then she checked her appointment book. It would be a full day tomorrow: a manicure and pedicure at ten a.m., and a hair appointment at noon.

When she checked her messages, she realized she had missed a call from Thomas. Since he went to sleep at 8 p.m. every night, she decided not to return his call. She was torn between wanting to hear what he had to say and calling his sister Mary, her best friend, to gossip as usual. Mary would fill her in on what had happened between Thomas and Maddie. It was something she had to know.

She sat at her vanity, brushing her hair and gazing in the mirror, remembering the day Thomas had carved their initials into the tree: T.S. + S.S. with a heart. They were in a part of the woods where the trees looked as if they had faces, and the trees were called *The Kissing Trees*. It was a beautiful day, with birds singing and a gentle breeze.

Mary had thrown her arms around a tree, pretending it was Eli, a boy she liked, but she'd never had a date with him. When she kissed the tree, Stephanie had laughed so hard that she fell over, rolling on the ground.

Stephanie gasped when Thomas and Eli stepped out from behind the foliage with broad smiles. She blushed bright pink. She'd had a crush on Thomas for months; sometimes she lay awake thinking about him. He was tall and lean, and ever so good-looking. When he chopped wood for her grandmother last fall, she'd stood at her bedroom window and watched his strong, muscular arms swing the ax.

Mary was laughing, but Stephanie grew quiet. The boys had seen them doing something foolish. Stephanie stood and began brushing the leaves off her dress.

Thomas had a wry smile, and his eyes were dancing. "So, you have found the 'Kissing Trees,' is that what you want, Stephanie Stratford, a kiss?"

"No, I don't!" Stephanie said, indignant, her hands on her hips.

"Well, I'm pretty good at it," he grinned. "I've got to be better than a tree."

Thomas took a step forward, and she took a step backward, then turned and ran. But he quickly caught up with her—grabbing her around the waist. They tumbled to the ground, and she lay looking up at his face, leaning over her on one elbow, his eyes dancing in amusement. He gazed at her with unconcealed interest, and his eyes roved over her slowly, landing on her rounded breasts. "How old are you now? Fourteen?" he asked casually.

"Fifteen," she sniffed. "You know how old I am, Thomas Shrock. I'm the same age as Mary."

"That's right, you are fifteen," he said, his gray eyes dancing. "I must say you've grown up nicely, Stephanie Stratford."

Her look was haughty. He'd caught her doing something stupid, and he knew perfectly well how old she was. He'd been coming to her birthday parties for years.

"Fifteen," he said again, seeming to ponder her age, as he leaned in closer, his lips inches from hers.

She could barely breathe, and closed her eyes, and waited—and waited...

And then he said, "You're an English girl—too young to be kissed. We must wait a year." He hopped up and pulled her to her feet.

"I'm not too young, Thomas Shrock," she said, her green eyes flashing. "And I don't know why you think I even want to kiss you."

Thomas had noticed that she was breathless and nervous. "I think you do," he said. "But we will wait because it's the proper thing to do. I wouldn't want to get on the wrong side of the Judge. When you're sixteen, we'll go to the river during Rumspringa, and we'll have our first kiss."

She was standoffish when Thomas took her hand and led her to the "kissing tree." Half-serious and half-joshing, he said, in with a clear German accent, as he'd heard the Bishops speak in the Old Amish Church, "I name this tree, Thomas Shrock. You must wait for me, and never kiss another tree."

The tendrils of the old oak swayed in the breeze as if it were giving its approval.

He took out his penknife, and she watched as she carved their initials on the giant oak tree—T.S. + S.S. She gave a faint smile, not willing to give in to her hidden emotions. *What is this tom-foolery?* She was impatient. Waiting months for a kiss was outrageous.

Suddenly, Mary and Eli came walking out of the woods. She gazed at Stephanie and said, "Eli's much better than a tree. But he talks too much when we should be kissing. I'll have to train him to be more like my tree." Her joy was short-lived when she noticed sadness in Stephanie's eyes. She turned to Thomas and said, "Why didn't you kiss her?"

"She's English, too young. The tree will have to do until she's sixteen, but I've carved our initials on the tree."

Mary frowned. "Well, I wouldn't wait too long. She's beautiful. A girl like her will have plenty of suitors."

It was one of her favorite memories of her and Thomas. She had gone back every year and traced her fingers over their initials in the tree. Every time she went back, she hugged the tree as if the tree were Thomas. Now that she was home, she had a different perspective. Memories of Thomas were harrowing, and her feelings for him ran deep. *A silly childhood crush*, she told herself, but her heart told her it was more.

Climbing into bed, she reached for the black book, but changed her mind. Thomas had been so convincing. The prince's face, still vivid in her memory, had unsettled her to the point of questioning her sanity. She opened her nightstand drawer, her hands trembling as she placed the book inside, and slammed it shut with a loud thud.

The image of the prince's face seemed to taunt her from the pages, mocking her, and she hated herself for believing in something so far-fetched. "It's just a fairy tale," she reassured herself.

Even though she had shut the book away, it didn't stop the dreams from coming.

Fireflies

Stephanie opened her eyes and stretched. She had slept longer than usual. Even though it was eight o'clock, fireflies came to mind. She closed her eyes and could see them, as well as the stars, and she could hear the rippling sounds of the river.

Someone was beside her—Thomas. She snuggled closer to him. Her heart pounded thinking about it. Life had been easy and carefree. Those were the best days when she didn't care what people thought—when being with Thomas under the stars was the most natural thing in the world. It didn't matter that she was a rich girl, and he was as poor as a church mouse. But college had changed everything with her and Thomas. If only she could go back to the way things used to be. She closed her eyes as the memory unfolded.

The tall, black, ornate iron gates swung open, and Stephanie drove the classic English Bentley through the gate and up the cobblestone drive lined with poplar trees.

To the side, a swinging sign with Old English letters read: Stratford Place, Judge Daniel Stratford, Owner. She was home for the summer and struck by the beauty of the elegant English-style house, Stratford Place. Summers were lovely, the house, set high on a hill, loomed over the countryside; an idyllic setting in a patchwork of colorful wildflowers and well-kept grounds.

She was going to Rumspringa tonight, despite her father's objections. All of her Amish friends would be there, and it would be Jacob's first Rumspringa. He had asked her to come, and she wanted to be part of it.

She had been unaware of Wizard Anzor's mystical, sharp blue eyes fixed upon her. He had sat high on a hill on the gnarled limb of a large oak tree in the middle of the expansive, manicured lawn. Had she looked, she might have seen Owl perched beside him.

Stephanie had breathed a sigh of relief when the iron gates closed behind her with a clang. After a grueling week of exams, she was ready to blow off some steam with friends. After the party, she planned to shut out the outside world and relax with a book within the confines of Brighton House. But there was also work to be done. The house was being renovated, and she wouldn't move in until winter, but there was a lot to do, and she planned to clean out closets and drawers. The palatial country estate was her refuge from the outside world and a place to go to get away from Marguerite, who was always looking over her shoulder.

On the drive, thoughts of the Rumspringa party consumed her. She had not seen Thomas for weeks, and she was there for Jacob, Thomas's younger brother. She had always tried to be there for birthdays and important events in his life. Jacob was sixteen, and it would be the first time that boundaries would be loosened; he would have his first beer and cigarette. And maybe even have his first kiss. Everyone knew Jacob had a secret crush on her; maybe Rumspringa would end it if he found a girl that he liked.

She shook herself from her daydream, glanced at the clock on the dashboard, and reminded herself to hurry or she would be late for the party. A glance in the rear-view mirror, as she drove up the winding drive, had told her that the circles under her eyes from weeks of studying were still there. Still, they were not as dark as they had been this morning. She had smoothed wisps of pale blonde hair that had loosened from her hairdo, and had wished that she had put ice on her eyes this morning.

Midway uphill, she stopped the old Bentley roadster and looked down over the green hillside at Brighton House. The house was hers, and she longed to go home, but her father had called and told her to go to Stratford Place.

"The house belongs to me now, Daddy. I want to go home," Stephanie protested. "That's the way my grandmother wanted it. You know, Marguerite and I don't get along."

"You're only eighteen, Steph. Too young to be on your own. Besides, the house is being renovated. It isn't ready to move in yet. Emily will be there to greet you—someone has to look after you while we are in Charleston over the summer. Now mind what I say and don't give your nanny a hard time."

Stephanie couldn't seem to draw herself away from the splendor of Brighton House. It looked lovely in the summer, set in the middle of tall pines and gigantic oaks; miles of white fence surround the twenty-acre estate, and a wide gate enunciates the two estates. A well-worn path called the Middle Path joined the two houses. She had walked that path hundreds of times growing up. There were so many memories here. It was her home, a place she never wanted to leave.

Emily had greeted her with a hug at the door and had an excellent lunch waiting for her: a honey ham sandwich, macaroni salad, and a generous piece of cherry pie with a cold glass of sun-brewed tea.

After chatting with Emily, she had gone upstairs to her old room to get ready for the Rumspringa party. She'd added some lavender salts to her bath water and had a relaxing soak. Then she put on a white chenille robe, sat at the vanity, and Emily brushed her hair.

"Your hair has grown four inches since I last trimmed it. It's past your waist. I'll sharpen my scissors, and we'll cut it when you come to quilt with Mary on Monday evening," Emily said. "Monday will be a busy day; it is wash day, but a special dinner and quilting in the evening will be relaxing."

"I think so, too," Stephanie said. "You don't need to fuss with my hair. Just put it in a chignon. It's hot and muggy."

"Are you sure you don't want to wear it down with a ribbon?" Emily asked as she ran the brush through her hair.

"Is Mary wearing her hair down tonight?" Stephanie asked.

"I don't think so. But Thomas mentioned he would like to see your hair down," Emily said. "He loves your long, blonde hair."

"Why would Thomas care? I thought he was dating Maddie Yoder," Stephanie asked, surprised. "I don't think I need to be concerned about what Thomas wants. Put it in a chignon."

Emily twisted her hair into a chignon and pinned it in place like she'd been doing for years. "Thomas has been miserable without you."

"I doubt it," Stephanie said. "I know about Maddie Yoder." She didn't want to pretend she didn't know with Emily. They'd always been honest with each other, but it didn't seem right to discuss Thomas with his mother. "How is it going with Eli and Mary?"

"Yes. Eli has been calling on Mary for several months. It's supposed to be a secret, but I've been busy, if you know what I mean."

Stephanie smiled. They kept weddings secret until right before the event and announced them at church. "I won't say a word."

"Mary told me once that you had your first kiss at Rumspringa," Stephanie said with a gleam in her eye.

"I did," Emily said, as a wave of nostalgia swept over her.

"What was it like?" Stephanie asked, intrigued.

"My heart jumped out of my chest, and I couldn't breathe," Emily said, as she brought her hand to her chest and laughed.

"Was it Fritz?" Stephanie asked, leveling her curious green eyes at Emily's as she watched her cheeks turn pink in the mirror's reflection.

"Of course, it was Fritz. He was the only man I have ever kissed, and the only man I ever wanted to kiss," Emily said with a dreamy look as she pinned Stephanie's chignon with hairpins.

"How did you know Fritz was the only one you ever wanted to kiss if you'd kissed no one else?" Stephanie asked. "How did you know Fritz was the one?"

"It's hard to describe; I had butterflies. My heart was beating so fast I thought he must hear it, and I didn't want him to stop kissing me."

"How old were you?" Stephanie asked.

"Sixteen. And Fritz was eighteen. We were married six months later and moved into a tiny house on his parents' big farm, and that's how we started. Thomas was born in the first year. Fritz wanted a baby every year, but we had to wait three years for Mary to come along. When the Judge asked me to be your nanny, I was so proud to have two babies. It was like having twins. I loved it. I would take you to church with me, and the ladies would pass you back and forth, raving about your blonde hair and fair skin."

"Marguerite and Daniel didn't like it when you spoke Pennsylvania Dutch. You picked up everything so fast. Three years later, Jacob came along, and you were only three, but you wanted to hold him, and I let you." Emily paused and laughed. "After you learned how to read, you taught Jacob how to read and taught him his numbers. And then Fritz complained because Jacob was sounding too English. You've spoiled him rotten throughout the years."

"I'm afraid I haven't been much of a sister to him this past year...with all that's happened," she said with a wistful expression. Avoiding the truth, she didn't want to say it—she'd fallen away from her Amish family when she had gone away to college.

Emily caught her by surprise when she said, "Rubin Yoder saw you walking with an older man when he was in the village picking up supplies. Thomas was upset when he heard."

"That was Aunt Clair's nephew, Hugh Grant. He's my English Literature professor. I thought Daddy told you I'd moved in with Aunt Clair. Hugh lives there, too. We often walk together. It was nothing," Stephanie said. "We're only friends."

Emily breathed a long sigh of relief. "I remember Clair Bartlett. She and Hedy were best friends. She used to come for tea during the summer. You always called her Aunt Clair."

"Yes. She's helped me a lot. Her boarding house is almost like being at home."

"Do you like your dress?" Emily asked, changing the subject.

"I love it. It's plain and loose-fitting. It will feel good in this muggy weather. Thank you for making it for me," Stephanie said. "You fuss over me too much."

"You are like my own, and I love fussing over you," Emily said. "Pale yellow is your color. As soon as I saw the material, I knew I had to make you a dress. I made Mary a blue one, but I copied your dress out of a Vogue magazine that I saw at Marguerite's."

Stephanie smiled. "You always make everything so special for me, Emily. When we go to Sugar Creek, I will buy you some material for a new dress. It's time you had something new. I'll cut it out for you, but I would be nervous about making it. I'm good at quilting, but I've never made a dress."

Emily laughed. "My closet is too full. But I need some thread if you insist on buying me something. I checked your sewing basket, and you need blue and peach. They have so many new colors now."

Again, the subject changed as Stephanie approached the delicate subject. "I thought I might stay at Brighton House tonight. I know it's being renovated, but there are six bedrooms. There must be one room that doesn't have sawdust in it." *There it was out in the open—she wanted to exert her independence and stay alone. After all, it was her house. Her grandmother had left it to her.*

"Judge thinks you're too young to stay alone, and old houses have a lot of creaks and noises. There's still a lot of work that needs to be done. The big oak outside of your bedroom window needs to be trimmed. Some limbs brush against the window. I'll stay with you here until Judge and Marguerite return from Charleston."

"You don't have to babysit me, Emily. I've been on my own at college, and I'm too tired to have the jitters. Besides, I want to sleep in tomorrow. After staying up late and studying for exams, I need to rest. Brighton House is my home, and it belongs to me."

Stephanie had butterflies in her stomach thinking about seeing Thomas again. When she arrived at the river, she saw her friend's horse and buggy parked in a row. She pulled her Bentley into the last one at the end of the row, where Thomas Shrock's horse, Betsy, stood chewing grass. Stephanie had grabbed an apple for Betsy from the kitchen before leaving; Betsy was crunching on the apple when Thomas walked up.

"Trying to get secrets out of my horse," Thomas joshed, hugging Stephanie.

"We girls have to stick together," she murmured, shaken by his closeness and good looks.

Maybe it was because she had not seen him for several weeks, but she thought him even more handsome than when they'd been together at her grandmother's funeral. He took her hand as if nothing had ever happened, and they fell into step. Fireflies had lit the way down the narrow, beaten path as they walked side by side to the clearing by the river.

Stephanie had been the last to arrive. As they approached, she could hear Eli Yoder talking nonstop about having his first beer, a Bud Light. Smoke filled the air, and it wasn't from the fire. A few were having their first cigarette tonight. They had saved their money for months and carried their beer and cigarettes in brown paper grocery bags from the Kroger store.

She smiled when she saw Jacob standing around the fire with a group of his friends, looking handsome and holding a beer. She could see he was attempting to be cavalier. He smiled a wry smile when he saw her.

Stephanie made a fuss over him. "You've grown so tall and good-looking, attempting to. And here you are having a beer. I suppose you're going to sow some wild oats tonight."

"That's what Rumspringa is about," he beamed. "I'm going to have my first kiss tonight."

"Who's the lucky girl?" Stephanie asked with a smile, looking around for the girl.

"You," he said, looking into her eyes. "Right here," he said, pointing to his cheek.

Everyone was staring at her, waiting for her reaction. Some guys were grinning and elbowing each other; she had to kiss him.

Jacob leaned down, and when she went to kiss him on the cheek, Thomas moved in front of him.

"Your first kiss will not be with my girl," Thomas said.

Jacob looked at Thomas with a broad smile and said with a dare, "I'll arm wrestle you for a kiss with your girl. What do you think about that?"

"I think you're getting too big for your britches, and I might have to bring you down a notch," Thomas said, stone-faced as he kicked at a log near the fire.

"Stephanie's a college girl now," Eli joshed as he popped a cold beer and handed it to Stephanie. "Maybe she doesn't want to be with us anymore."

Stephanie was already feeling a little shy because she and Thomas had parted on uncertain terms before she'd left for college. She tipped the bottle to her lips and let the beer stream down her throat. Feeling their stares, she said, "Of course I want to be with you. Nothing's changed."

Her friends seemed to be relieved at her answer.

They roasted marshmallows and hot dogs on long, sharpened branches and talked about everything imaginable, but Thomas's big barn apartment was the main topic of conversation. Even though it had happened months ago, the boys still liked to talk about it. It was the most enormous barn they'd ever raised. There had been seventy-five young, strapping Amish men who raised the barn in two days.

Stephanie was glad to be back with her friends and away from the pressures of college. She felt relaxed as they sat around the blazing fire, eating hot dogs and marshmallows, talking about everything under the sun. As dusk turned to dark, the lanterns were lit, and Jacob and his friends went down by the river to skip flat rocks. One of them had brought a boom box, and the sounds of country western music filled the night air.

Romance was in the air. After a while, couples paired off with their quilts to find their spot, a secluded place where they could be alone. She had felt a nervous rush when Thomas took her by the arm and led her down the well-worn path. Familiar sounds had filled the starlit night; crickets chirped, frogs croaked, and she could hear the ripple of the river. They passed by burning red embers of cigarettes, and she could hear the soft murmurings of her friends in the night.

For the first time in weeks, they found themselves alone. Stephanie had butterflies in her stomach as Thomas spread the dark blue, hand-stitched quilt that Emily had made for her when she was sixteen years old.

"I thought we would stargaze tonight," Stephanie said, trying to ease the tension. "We used to stargaze a lot when we were young."

"We used to do a lot of things," Thomas said. "Do you want another beer?"

"A beer would be nice."

"I suppose you've had a lot of these at college. That's what college girls do, isn't it?"

"I've blown off a little steam after exams. But not too much now that I'm not in the dormitory. I spend a lot of time with Aunt Clair. It's like having Hedy back."

Thomas popped two beers in the moonlight, handed one to her, and sat down beside her on the quilt. "I heard you've been spending time with Claire's nephew, a college professor," Thomas said, not mincing words.

"We're friends. Nothing more," Stephanie said, swallowing hard, glad that he could not see her burning cheeks in the dark. She tipped her beer to her lips and let it stream down her throat. The night was muggy, and she was feeling uncomfortable from both the humidity and the conversation.

She fidgeted with her dress and sighed. It felt strange coming back to the river after being away at college. Thomas had been her crush, but it made her nervous the way he was acting as if he was going to reveal his feelings for her—and worse yet—act on them.

"Let down your hair," he whispered. "I love your long, blonde hair." Then he had lain back on one elbow and watched her.

"It's too hot," she said, pushing a wisp of hair away from her face.

Thomas set his jaw and gave her a look. "Come on—I thought you were my girl."

Stephanie blushed, pulled the pins out of her hair, and let it fall down her back onto the blanket. When he reached over to smooth it, a shiver went down her spine.

A full moon had cast a luminous light over the fair, beautiful girl, and she lay back beside him. Her hair had spread over the hand-stitched quilt that Thomas' mother, Emily, had made for her. In the moonlight, with her luminous porcelain face and blush lips, she had looked surreal, as if she were a fairy princess.

She could feel Thomas' eyes drinking her in as her eyes roved over his tall, lean body. When his eyes roamed over her breasts, she felt self-conscious and crossed her arms over her chest.

An owl screeched, and Stephanie sat up, her eyes searching for the creature. He was nowhere to be seen, but she knew it was Owl. He followed her everywhere. It brought her attention to the sky.

"There must be a thousand stars, Thomas." When her words were met with silence, she reached over and grabbed his arm and shook him. "Thomas, you aren't listening. I've found The Big Dipper." She extended her arm and pointed her finger into the sky. When their eyes met, he did not look like a boy, but a man with powerful emotion and passion in his face.

Thomas looked up at the sky. "I have other things on my mind."

"What?"

"We're not kids anymore. I'm a grown man, Stephanie, and you're a woman. It's time we kissed." His gray eyes searched hers. "Haven't you ever thought about it?"

Stephanie heaved a sigh. She was a virgin. Everyone in the county knew that Stephanie Stratford had never had a date and had never been kissed. Her father intimidated boys who had an interest in her. His scowl alone was enough to deter them.

"Maybe," she said. Glad that he could not see her flush in the dark. The truth of the matter was — she'd thought about it a lot, but now she was having second thoughts.

His arm went around her. "You've never been kissed," he whispered. "I'll teach you." He pulled her to him, and she felt his breath on her neck.

Her heart was pounding.

She closed her eyes in expectation, her lips trembling.

She felt his warm breath on her ear as he whispered, "I've waited months for this moment."

The owl screeched again, and Stephanie started. She wasn't squeamish, but there was something about the screech that frightened her. And then came the chilling whinny call repeated over and over that made her blood run cold. It was a warning.

Stephanie jumped to her feet.

There was a rustling in the brush. As her eyes adjusted to the dark, she saw Owl's huge yellow eyes staring at her.

"I have to go," she said, running down the path to the roadster. She jumped in the car, breathless, and drove away, screeching her tires. Owl spread his wings and flew behind her.

At the river, the moon shone upon the silhouette of Thomas as he watched the red taillights of the car fade away.

Stephanie smiled as she came out of the daydream. It was a pleasant memory— being in Thomas' arms in the moonlight. He used to call her his girl, though they had never kissed.

First Kiss

Three days later, after Becca left for the day, Stephanie checked the drawing room and foyer to make sure everything was in order. The room looked warm and inviting after she polished the furniture that morning. She turned on the tree lights and stood back, admiring the tree.

Satisfied that everything was in order, Stephanie hurried upstairs to get ready. Brooks followed at her heels, carrying a bone she had given him earlier. His thick golden coat shone. She had dropped him off at the groomer before she got her nails and hair done.

It had been a long day, and she soaked in a hot bath with lavender salts, almost drifting off. She applied her makeup with a faint dusting of blush with a sable brush, a light shade of berry lip gloss that made her lips look full and luscious, and a scant amount of mascara to her already thick lashes. She held out her hands, admiring her French manicure, then applied hand lotion.

"Perfect," she said to Brooks, who was lying near her feet.

When she put on the black dress and looked in the mirror, she almost didn't recognize the sophisticated girl who looked back at her. Her silky hair hung long and straight over one shoulder. Her diamond earrings sparkled—rich and elegant. Earlier, she had gone to the safe and selected a sapphire ring and a diamond. She slipped the rings on her fingers and checked herself in the mirror. Then she took the diamond ring off, looked at it lovingly, and put it back in the velvet case. Not wanting to appear that she was flaunting her wealth, she took it downstairs to the safe in the library and locked it up securely. For a girl who didn't wear jewelry, two rings seemed like too many.

Last, she went into her grandmother's closet and pulled down a pair of silver heels, grateful that they wore the same size. She slipped them on and danced around in front of the mirror. They were perfect and felt wonderful on her feet. Her father thought it macabre, and hated it when she wore her grandmother's clothes. But her grandmother had great taste, and her clothes were expensive. She couldn't bear to give them away. It seemed silly not to wear them.

When the doorbell rang, she froze. She looked at the clock in Hedy's room and realized she'd lost track of time. She ran into the drawing room, glanced out the window, and saw a sleek, black limo.

"Oh, my God," she said, taking a deep breath. Her heels clicked down the wooden hall to the foyer. She was nervous, not knowing what to expect. There seemed to be a million butterflies in her stomach when she opened the door and looked into smiling, steel-blue eyes.

Richard wore a black tux and black bow tie. Everything about him looked meticulous. He took her breath away. He was seven years older, but the age difference seemed to have disappeared. She had not remembered his shoulders being that broad. When he hugged her, she felt a pull of magnetic attraction.

He held her away by her shoulders, giving her a long, penetrating look. "You are gorgeous. I can't take my eyes off you."

She blushed.

"Thank you. And thank you for the roses. They're beautiful."

She took his hand and led him into the drawing room, and gestured towards the roses displayed on the piano. But he wasn't looking at the roses; he couldn't seem to break his gaze from her face.

Their parents were best friends, and they had been socializing together all their lives. She'd danced with him at the Christmas Party when she was sixteen. She had been in awe of him that night. There was a warm familiarity between them, but she had not expected the undercurrent of physical attraction.

"Would you like a drink?" she asked, even though she did not know how to mix a drink.

"No, we should go. The driver is waiting." He helped her on with her coat. "I feel like a fool. We should have met months ago."

"I've only been home from college for a few days. I doubt I would have had time. There's been so much to do—with getting ready for Christmas."

"Well, the place looks great. It's warm and inviting, as if you've always lived here. I love your tree."

"I *have* always lived here. Brighton House is home to me. I'll give you a tour later."

"There's nothing I would like better. Leave a light on; we won't be back till late."

In the limo's backseat, a shiver shot up her spine. Not from the cold, but from the thrill of Richard's unexpected touch when his cool hand brushed against her leg.

"You look stunning," he whispered, his lips near her ear. "I'll be jealous the entire night."

Flattered, she looked up at him, her green eyes dancing with excitement. "No worries. You're the only man I want to be with tonight. The roses were unexpected. Do you always do such sweet things?"

"I sent you the roses for a reason," he said with a wry smile. "You hated me when we were children; I have scars from your baby teeth."

Stephanie laughed, "I don't remember biting you. You didn't have to send the roses."

"There's more," he chided. "It didn't get better. You didn't like me at all when you were ten. I beat you at chess, and you kicked me under the table." He laughed. "I'll never forget it. You were a demure, beautiful child, and looked like such a little lady, dressed up in pinafores with ribbons in your hair. But damned, those patent leather shoes hurt!"

She loved his sense of humor and everything about him, and didn't dare tell him he had captivated her from the first moment their eyes had met. She would have forgiven him for anything. He was outrageously handsome, a

Matthew McConaughey look-alike, dashing and exciting, unlike any man she had ever met.

His blue eyes were intense. "I've been waiting a long time for this date, and it was worth the wait."

"I didn't know. Daddy said nothing until recently."

"I think he was worried that I might distract you from your studies. You're lovely."

Her eyes shone with flirtation. "Thank you. You are very handsome." She felt like Cinderella on her way to the ball.

"I've been here hundreds of times, but it's never looked this lovely," she said as they drove up the winding drive. Thousands of white lights sparkled on the tall, full, snow-flocked spruce trees, and candles cast a soft glow on the windows.

They could hear the carolers as the sleek black limo neared the ominous gray stone building. It was bitterly cold when Richard helped her out, but she smiled and tucked her arm in his. The towering double doors decorated with massive Victorian evergreen and holly wreaths looked welcoming. They hesitated for a moment to listen to the singing. Then he whisked her inside out of the raw, wintry air.

As soon as her silver slippers crossed the threshold onto the gleaming marble floor, she felt as if she were in the middle of a fairy tale with her prince charming. Two life-size nutcracker dolls met them, and a flocked blue spruce Christmas tree, decorated with huge shiny bulbs, went all the way to the ceiling. She beamed up at Richard. "In German tradition, the toy soldiers are symbols of good luck. They scare away evil spirits."

Richard squeezed her hand. "There are no evil spirits here, darling. I feel like the luckiest man in the world to be here with you." They stood holding hands, looking up at the tree, oblivious to everyone around them. "Next year, I'll take you to the ballet in New York to see The Nutcracker. I go every year."

She smiled up at him, feeling a pang of nostalgia because she'd gone to The Nutcracker with her grandmother many times. She hadn't gone since, though her father and Marguerite went every year and always invited her.

Dazzling five-tiered crystal chandeliers cast a warm, inviting glow, as the sound of a ten-piece orchestra playing "Silver Bells" filled the air, lending to the jovial mood of the guests. It was the party that everyone looked forward to all year, and the guests were dancing as if there were no tomorrow. Stephanie felt at ease as they moved down the red-carpeted, vast hall to the ballroom with her arm tucked into Richard's. They walked along, extending greetings to their friends. They'd both grown up in Brier Hill County and knew the same people. She saw the women's envious expressions, and she was aware of admiring glances from men.

When they reached the Victorian Christmas tree where their parents were waiting, her father hugged her, and she kissed her father on the cheek and whispered, "He is so… good looking. And he's funny. I don't know why I worried." Her father nodded. She thought he had a melancholy expression.

"Richard is an extraordinary man," Daniel said. "We'd always hoped to bring the two of you together." Though he said it, Stephanie had heard a twinge of loss in his voice.

"You couldn't lose her to a better man," Parker joshed as he patted Daniel on the back. Exuding self-confidence and charisma, Richard chimed in, "I agree."

Marguerite's dark eyes scrutinized Stephanie. "This is the first year I haven't picked out your dress for the Christmas party. I bought your gowns in Charleston. But I have to admit, the dress is you—elegant and rich. Hedy's diamond earrings go well with the dress. She would be proud."

Stephanie's fingers touched the earrings. "They aren't Hedy's. Daddy got me these last year for Christmas." A look passed between the two. Marguerite had always said Daniel spoiled her rotten.

Richard's mother, Marsha, quickly changed the subject. "You are positively glowing. We need pictures. Where's the photographer?"

Richard stepped between them. "Not now, Mother. You're smothering her. Let her catch her breath."

Servers stood by with silver trays of champagne flutes. She was nervous when Richard handed her a flute, and their eyes met. He was looking at her mouth as if he wanted to kiss her. It made her uncomfortable because she'd never been kissed.

Parker lifted his glass and gave a toast. "To Stephanie and Richard—may their future together be as bright as this Christmas tree."

Stephanie smiled, her hand trembling as she clinked her glass to Richard's. She took a sip. When she looked up and her eyes met Richard's, she knew what was coming—his lips were warm and tender, and she thought her heart would beat right out of her chest.

"That was my first kiss," she said in a soft voice.

"Why did we wait so long?" Richard asked. "I've wanted to kiss you from the first moment I laid eyes on you tonight."

She was young and naïve and felt heady and intoxicated when he led her to the dance floor and kissed her again. His kisses were heart-stopping. It was an understatement to say Richard had swept her off her feet. A whirlwind of emotions engulfed her. She was in a room full of people, shy about returning his ardor.

Stephanie was aware of Richard's reputation with women and that he'd left a string of broken hearts when he left for college. It was foolhardy to believe a man could fall in love with her this fast, and she reminded herself to guard her heart. Thomas had hurt her terribly. Falling in love with Richard might prove equally painful.

Mistletoe

Richard was fun-loving and charming. They mingled around the reindeer ice sculpture, chatting with friends. Then they went to the chocolate bar and tasted the delicious chocolate. They had a lovely dinner with their family at an enormous round table with a centerpiece of candles, pine, and vivid red berries. He was attentive, ordering an expensive wine that he thought she would like at dinner, sending back her steak when it was too rare, and while the orchestra played music, everyone loved it.

Richard requested a particular song: "My Love" by Lionel Richie. It was the first song they'd ever danced to, and the words suited them romantically. Stephanie dropped her guard. Her heart pounded when he kissed her under the mistletoe.

The Country Club socialites loved a good romance, and the men said joining old money together was never a bad thing. It appeared to the country-club set that the tight-knit Coopers and Stratfords—two of the most distinguished families in Brier Hill County—had assured the future of the next generation.

A woman in Marguerite's bridge club whispered to her friend, "Maybe Stephanie will forget about that nice-looking Amish man now."

"Or not," the other woman cajoled. "Maybe she will have two lovers."

Stephanie knew of the stares and whispers. It was a small town, and the Stratfords and the Coopers were the most prominent families in Brier Hill

County. She had connected the dots; her father and Parker were quite the matchmakers. She was sure that Marguerite and Marsha had been in on it, too. No one could have predicted the immediate attraction.

They had just danced the last dance. Richard was whispering, his gaze riveted on her. "All I want to do is get you alone."

"That's not possible," she said. "My parents are having an after-party. I always help Marguerite."

When her father strode over and said, "Time to go home, Cinderella, it's almost midnight," Richard's complexion changed to red around the collar.

Stephanie laughed. "Have you forgotten? I came with Richard. Shouldn't Richard decide when it's time to leave?"

Marsha broke the tension as she took Stephanie's arm. "There's a new tree I want you to see. It's called the 'Sugar and Spice' tree. It's decorated with dolls, tinsel, sugar cookies, and candies. I thought of you as soon as I saw it. It could be your first Christmas tree in your new home."

"A 'Sugar and Spice,' tree," Richard mused. "Stephanie already has a Christmas tree. It's beautiful. I don't think she needs another one."

Daniel put his arm on Richard's shoulder. "Stephanie can have more than one tree. Marguerite has a Christmas tree in almost every room of the house. She loves decorating. Women love that sort of thing."

Marsha took Stephanie's arm and led her away. "I've always wanted a daughter. I know you are busy with Brighton House, but I would love to decorate this tree with you. It reminds me of you and your love for fairy tales. It even has an owl."

Stephanie stood starry-eyed, looking up at the tree and what must have been a thousand decorations. "I love it," she said. "But there's not much time before Christmas." It was then that Stephanie thought of Thomas and felt a sinking feeling. She had hoped to have Thomas's family over for dinner before Christmas and exchange gifts. There wasn't much time. "I'm not sure," she stammered. "Maybe we should do it next year."

"Nonsense," Marsha said. "It won't take long. We'll do it this week. Marguerite said you put up a tree using your grandmother's decorations. The Sugar and Spice tree will be your creation—something different from your grandmother's. Richard's assistant, Bradley Taylor, enjoys outdoor activities. I'm sure he would be happy to cut your tree."

"Okay, we'll do the tree," Stephanie said, giving in—though she didn't know when she would find the time.

She felt Daniel's arm on her shoulder. "Your pumpkin and four white mice await you," he said in a teasing voice. It was all-encompassing—and she felt pulled in two different directions. She thought her father looked tired. The night had gone by in a blur. She looked around for Richard, and he was talking to a friend.

When the orchestra stopped playing, people left, and she heard Marguerite call out in a champagne-laden voice, "Grab a centerpiece. They'll go to waste if we don't take them."

"Old habits never die," Daniel complained. "You have too many centerpieces, Marguerite."

"I need them for the Christmas tours," she protested. "You can be such a Scrooge when you get tired. It will only take a minute."

Marsha nudged Stephanie. "Grab one. It will make your mother happy."

Stephanie looked around for a bouquet. When she turned on her heel to fetch it, she ran right smack into Blaine Miller, a friend of Thomas's. Amish often worked in the kitchen during parties. He was carrying a tray of dirty glasses, and she'd almost caused him to drop them. He had looked away, as if it embarrassed him to look at her. She looked down at her dress, self-conscious.

She knew at that moment that everything she'd done would be all over Brier Hill County tomorrow. It occurred to her she hadn't had closure with Thomas, and he would hear about this tomorrow, but she didn't care. She had suffered a hard blow from Thomas, and it would serve him right.

She had to have one last look at the 'Sugar and Spice' tree. Her eyes traveled from the top of the tree to the window at the top of the wall. Her jaw dropped—Owl's large yellow eyes fixed on her unblinking, and when his head spun, an eerie feeling swept over her. She was sure it was a bad omen, as if he were sending her a warning. She swayed, and Richard caught her—just in time.

"Are you okay, honey? You look like you saw a ghost."

Her voice was a faint whisper. "Owl was in the window, but he's gone."

"It was probably just a shadow—a tree branch waving in the wind," Richard said, hiding his surprise that an owl had caused so much distress. "Wait for me here. Mother needs help to carry some things."

She didn't wait because she wanted to see if Owl was still there on the ledge. When the doorman opened the door for her, the snow was blowing and drifting like a blizzard, making it difficult to see.

Stephanie heard a rustle above her as Owl—huge and ominous — flew off the ledge of the old stone building, swooping down so close she felt the wind from his wings. She jumped back, terrified, and that's when she fell—and her silver slipper came off and flew into the air. She watched as Owl grabbed up the slipper in his beak and soared up into the dark sky, his wingspan at least five feet wide.

Carter William's big hand reached down to pull her up. "Are you okay?" he asked.

"I'm okay," she said, "but Owl took my slipper. I feel terrible. It was Hedy's."

Carver had been their family driver for as long as she could remember and knew about Owl. She sensed his uneasiness as he helped her into the limo. She grabbed Carver's sleeve. "Don't tell Daddy about the slipper. It was Hedy's slipper, and it would only upset him."

"I've always kept your secrets, Ms. Stephanie, from the time you were knee high to a grasshopper. I won't say a word to your father, but don't fret about it. The slipper is gone forever, and you can't get it back. Sit tight. You're wet. I'll fetch some towels from the kitchen."

Looking up into the dark sky, hoping to glimpse Owl, she squinted. When she saw two white horses in front of the limo, her imagination ran rampant. She'd lost her slipper. Maybe the limo really would turn into a pumpkin with four white mice. She started when Richard jumped into the limo.

"I told you to wait," he said. "Carver told me what happened. He gave me these towels." He rubbed her feet briskly.

"It was frightening," she said, peering out the window. "Are there white horses standing in front of the limo… or am I imagining things?"

"Amish horses got loose," Richard replied. "They're rounding them up now."

She felt a little silly. The incident with Owl had been sobering, and she was not much in the mood for the after-party. All she wanted to do was go home and curl up in front of the fireplace with Richard, but she knew it would upset her father if they didn't go.

Her mind was on the slipper in the limo on the drive home. It held so much sentimental value, and now she felt guilty for wearing it. She'd turned around several times to see if Owl was following the limo. He lived in the rafters in the barn. Tomorrow she would go to the barn and look for the slipper.

As the limo headed down the drive following a convoy of limos headed for the after-party, she snuggled close in Richard's arms. The roads were icy and dark on the county road, but she trusted Carver's driving. There was a lot of kissing. She'd never made out before and was worried about what Carver would think when the windows steamed. He didn't seem to notice. He kept his eyes on the road.

When her eyes glimpsed the light, she realized they were at the entrance to Stratford Place and was relieved to see the big iron gate swing open. Her eyes followed the red taillights of at least ten limos going up the winding drive, intermixed with SUVs and sports cars. Tall pines decorated with white lights lined the drive. There were Christmas trees with hundreds of lights in almost every window of the mansion, evergreen wreaths on the doors, and big red bows on the gateposts. In the driveway, there was a flurry of activity, carrying appetizers and centerpieces into the house.

The frosty air bit at Stephanie's cheeks, and it reminded her she was missing a shoe. Richard swept her up in his arms and carried her into the house. While Richard went to help bring in the centerpieces, Stephanie padded up the steps to her old room. She found a pair of pink slippers in the closet, smoothed her hair, and put on lip gloss.

Then went to the window and looked out into the night, wishing with all of her might that Owl would bring the slipper back. She hurried downstairs to see if she could help, hoping no one would notice she was wearing old, worn house slippers.

Revenge

The great horned owl flew home to the Kingdom of Sirius- the Dog Star. The brightest star in all the universe. He had soared through the inky night, becoming nervous and fearful as he approached the magnificent medieval structure—Ludwig Castle.

Snow-capped mountains bounded the spiral, coned, magnificent castle and created a surreal, fairy tale apparition on a high, rocky cliff. Beneath, a roaring ocean with mountainous waves threatened to climb the jagged cliff. A full moon and bright stars illuminated the castle, and the small, quaint village of Wicket appeared in the distance, a few miles away. Below, scattered about, were a few small cottages with colorful red roofs and shutters. It was a welcoming sight—and it relieved him to be home after his long journey. He had rehearsed his speech well, for he would be the bearer of bad news.

Owl had seen the form of Prince Damien as he stood by the window. He was a princely man, but could be dark and foreboding if anyone dared to cross him. The window flung open wide, and Owl's expansive wings cleared the window, and with a swoosh, he flew into the stately study and dropped the silver shoe at Damien's feet. The slipper landed on the soft carpet unscathed.

Damien smiled and grabbed up the slipper and gazed at it, imagining the girl who had worn it. He dreamed of her nightly and had been awaiting Owl's arrival with news of his betrothed. Raven had arrived earlier and told of his coming.

The monkey climbed up Damien's vestments of breeches and brocades until he was sitting on his shoulder. He craned his neck, his big dark eyes locked on the slipper.

The library, furnished with eighteenth-century furnishings and paneled with rich, dark oak, was elegant. Ornate drapes of crimson velvets and rich brocades hung from the windows. A library of bound books lined two walls, and a roaring fire burned in the massive fireplace. Luminous shadows danced over the wall from the light of silver candlesticks. Renaissance art hung throughout the room. The faces in the paintings of those who had lived before seemed to come alive. They, too, had looked expectant as they awaited news about the young girl.

Owl landed on the heavy, wooden, oak perch Damien had made especially for him. He had attempted composure worthy of a great horned owl, but his nerves overtook him, and his head had spun.

Frightened by Owl's head spinning, the monkey had cowered and jumped to the floor. He threw his tiny arms around Damien's white leggings and screeched, "Make him stop! Make him stop."

Damien reached down, picking up the small monkey and stroking his back to calm him. "What is it, Owl? What has happened?"

Owl found his voice, but his words seemed much too loud, too deep. "Stephanie attended a Christmas party tonight, and a mortal kissed her."

Damien's face—once calm—had contorted with rage, and fire flamed from his nostrils. "She's mine," he cried out, sending echoes throughout the cavernous castle. "Wizard promised her to me."

Snitch shrieked in fear, and Owl drew back, spreading his expansive wings to maintain balance. Raven peered out from a dark corner.

It was as if a dagger had plunged into Damien's heart. "No other man shall have her. I will not allow it," he lashed out. "Lillian is planning our wedding, and I've searched the world for jewels to adorn her and filled the castle with art."

"She is exquisite, and the mortal is very handsome," Owl said. "The Seal of the Blushing Rose has fallen away. Many men will want her."

"Do you not think me worthy of such a creature?" Damien ranted. "Am I not generous enough to you, my friends, servants, and the people of Wicket?"

"You are kind, sire." Owl lied. "Most of the time," he uttered under his breath. "It is not you but Blood Eyes who carries out the cruel and heinous whippings and torture."

Damien tapped his pointing stick as he stood staring at Owl, his chiseled jaw twitching. Then he turned and went to the window, looking out at the waves thrashing against the cliff. The weather fit his mood.

Owl sat on his perch, staring straight ahead. Without Damien's eyes on him, he found the courage needed to speak. "Even the Wizard cannot make your hearts beat as one, sire."

Damien's dark eyes flashed. "Am I not handsome enough for her, Owl? Is that what you're saying?" he asked, striking the stone fireplace hard with the stick. He straightened his shoulders and stared hard at Owl. "Are you oblivious to the Wizard's powers? Have you forgotten that when she drinks the wine from the Chalice on our wedding day, she will lose all memory of earth?"

Owl puffed his feathers. "It's just that—what do you know of love, sire? You have only had wenches."

"You must remember, Owl, I did not choose to love her. I knew nothing of love until the Wizard gave her to me. What greater gift could I have—the girl with the golden ribbon, born perfect? Once the Wizard allowed me a glimpse of her through the crystal ball, I suffer daily wanting her. Your news has brought me more suffering." Damien's words were sharp and poignant. "I must make my presence known to her."

"Are you willing to give up your wenches for her, sire? The girl will not understand."

Damien looked pained. "My wenches comfort me and give me pleasure. I would be a fool to give them up."

"A twentieth-century girl may not be what you need. She's causing you more pain than pleasure. I regret it was I who brought such heart-wrenching news to you, sire," Owl said in a small voice, his yellow eyes luminous and vast.

"My black heart longs to possess her. I assure you I will love her, provide for her every need, and grant her every wish."

Attuned to Damien's feelings, Snitch said, "Have some ale and nuts, Master. That will make you feel better, and I will dance for you and play the tambourine."

"There is no time for you to dance for me tonight, Snitch, but I will call for Nettles to bring you your nuts and ale. No worries for you, my little pet," Damien said, stroking Snitch's back.

Owl puffed his feathers. He had flown through a portal, endured heavy winds, a meteor shower, and a snowstorm to bring Damien the slipper, and it was Snitch whom Damien rewarded. The dancing monkey did little to earn his keep. Owl knew what was wrong. Damien demanded complete servitude.

"I am your loyal servant, sire, and will do whatever you wish," Owl said obediently.

Damien smiled broadly. "You've had a long journey. I will send Raven to do the deed."

Owl shivered. Raven carried out evil deeds.

"Revenge lies heavy on my heart, and I will use my powers to thwart all attempts for her to love any mortal man. I will not allow it," Damien said as he sat down in a tall red chair in front of the blazing fire. Snitch jumped up into his lap. "Wizard will create the Black Snake Ribbon Spell," Damien stared into the fire as if hypnotized by the flames. "Raven will drop the black ribbon in the path of my beloved, and when she picks it up, it will coil around her like a snake and awaken the spell that will awaken doubt in her heart. Doubt—the great destroyer of dreams."

"Sire, I beg you to reconsider," Owl said, pleading. "Stephanie has done nothing to deserve such harsh treatment."

Damien sneered. "And I have done nothing to deserve the pain that I feel, knowing she has been with another." His eyes smoldered with hate as he examined the silver slipper in his hand. "The sight of the silver slipper gives me pain. I should burn it."

"Vengeance cannot ease your pain, sire. Vengeance can confuse a man's mind and soul to the point where he may not be sure of who he is avenging. — William Shakespeare, Hamlet."

Damien threw the slipper onto the thick wool rug, and it landed on its side undamaged. Besotted with pain and anger, Damien thundered, "You dare challenge me with Shakespeare's words. I could very well put you in the High Tower and chain you to your perch. You believe I cannot love the girl with the golden ribbon because I have never been in love. It is true—I know nothing of love, but I've felt its sting."

A dark shadow fell over the handsome Prince, and he went to the window, folded his arms, and looked out at the raging ocean. "Henceforth, I shall be darker than my brother Lucifer. I will create spells and use black magic on the girl born perfect — until I feel the touch of her sweet lips on mine."

Owl skittered back and forth across the perch. "Please do not become like your brother. I cannot carry the black ribbon and drop it. I love her. My conscience would not allow me to do such a thing."

"No, it will be Raven," Damien said. "His heart is black like mine."

Snitch shook his tambourine, and jingles cut through the tension-filled room. "Please don't become like Lucifer. I will dance and play my tambourine, and you will be happy."

Damien patted Snitch's head.

"You spoil him, Master. His character is despicable. He eavesdrops, spreads gossip all over the castle, and will steal anything bright and shiny. Yet you reward him with German ale and Brazil nuts every night. Don't you tire of a dancing monkey with a nightly tambourine performance?"

"Snitch is a bit of a simpleton, but he's loyal and entertaining," Damien said, unaffected.

Snitch eyed the gold ring around Owl's talon.

"You've had a long journey, Owl. Now you must eat, drink, and rest. Have a fat mouse. I'll send Raven to do the deed."

Raven had listened to Damien's every word from his perch in the shadows. He flew to Damien's shoulder, his beady, dark bird eyes alert.

"Go now, Raven, and fetch Wizard," Damien ordered. "There is much to do."

Revenge

Snitch eyed the silver slipper and crept across the floor, snatched it up, and held it to his chest. He would hide it away with his bright and shiny pretties.

Floozy

Stephanie awoke to the sunlight shining brightly on the pale-yellow floral wallpaper. Its gentle rays warmed the room. It had been an enchanting night, and Stephanie smiled, savoring the memory of Richard's kisses. Lying back on the pillow, she pulled the comforter up to her chin, luxuriating in the snug coziness.

She had a faint headache, and when the phone rang, she let the call roll over to the answering machine. Thomas's voice was clear and intense, as if he were standing right next to the bed. "Pick up the phone, Steph. I know you're there."

Barely breathing, she waited for him to hang up, but patience was one of his many virtues, and the click didn't come. Guilt slowly crept in as memories of last night filled her head. Maybe she shouldn't have let things go so far with Richard before breaking it off with Thomas. Everything had happened lightning fast with Richard. She couldn't talk to Thomas—not yet. She realized at that moment that she wasn't sure about anything at all.

"We have to talk, Steph," Thomas said. At last, there was a click. She exhaled, profoundly relieved.

It was nine o'clock, she'd overslept, and her body was screaming for a cup of tea, but she showered first, letting the hot water massage her neck and back to relax her muscles, hoping to relieve her headache. Then she threw on a chenille bathrobe, not taking the time to dress.

She put on the teapot and checked on Brooks and Boots. Brooks was asleep on a rug in the drawing-room, and Boots was sunning on the wide windowsill. Stephanie leaned over Boots and squinted into the bright sun at her parents' house—the Coopers' car was still there, but Richard's was not. She guessed they were having breakfast together and was relieved they hadn't called.

She didn't want to think about Richard while Thomas was in her head, but couldn't keep him out. Richard had been incredibly romantic. During the after-party at her parents' house, they'd mixed with the guests and made polite conversation. Then, he whisked her away to a dark corner in a small sitting area, and they'd swayed to the music with their bodies molded together in a downright indecent way. Eventually, Parker came to fetch them. They had never been entirely alone, and this morning she was glad because she needed time to sort things out.

While she ate a simple breakfast of tea, toast, and yogurt, she vacillated on calling Thomas. She was sure Blaine had already spilled his guts to Thomas by now. But Thomas had done much worse. Becca had said he'd gone to the barn with Maddie Yoder, and it weighed heavily on her mind. She would be lying to herself if she said she wasn't jealous. Even though she'd fallen hard for Richard, she still had feelings for Thomas.

After cleaning up the breakfast dishes, she poured herself another cup of tea and went upstairs. Her reflection showed circles under her eyes as she brushed her long hair and braided it in a snake braid. She put cold compresses on her eyes, then dressed in a pair of faded blue jeans and an old sweatshirt. When she went downstairs, Brooks was standing at the window, looking out and whining. He wanted to go for a walk, and she needed fresh air. She grabbed a fleece-lined red plaid coat and put on a scarf and gloves.

Brooks shot out when she opened the door. Even though the sunshine had gone, Stephanie walked down the cobblestone driveway. The chilly wind whipped at her face, and her breath frosted. The wind picked up as the clouds grew dark. The sleet stung her face, forcing her to turn around. As she picked up her pace, she called out to Brooks and pulled her red wool scarf around her face. She didn't see the tall figure coming towards her. He grabbed her arm, and she screamed.

Thomas looked at her hard.

"Oh, my God. You scared me, Thomas," she stammered, trying to regain her composure. She hadn't seen his buggy, but then she realized she had come out of the front door. He must have arrived as she was leaving for her walk.

"Why aren't you answering my calls?" he asked in a harsh voice. "I've called you half a dozen times, both last night and this morning."

"You knew I would be at the annual Christmas Party at the Country Club," Stephanie said. "I go with my family every year."

"You didn't leave here with your family last night. You left with Richard Cooper in a limo. I heard all about it from Blaine Miller. He told me you looked like a hussy and had rouged your face."

His words were more biting than the wind. Stephanie leveled her gaze at him. "Blaine exaggerated."

The silence between them was uncomfortable as they went inside and took off their boots and heavy coats in the mudroom. Thomas broke the reticence. "The house feels cold. You let the fire go out."

He brushed by her and entered the drawing-room. She glowered from the doorway with her arms folded and watched him stoke the hot coals. When he threw some kindling on the coals, the flames blazed.

"I'm sorry, Thomas. I'll put the kettle on for tea."

The steaming tea gurgled as Stephanie poured two mugs and then set them on coasters. She slid into the chair and waited for Thomas, unsure of what she would say. She began fidgeting with her hands and realized she was still wearing the emerald ring—another reminder of last night. Thomas, like all Amish, abhorred jewelry, thinking it pretentious. She didn't want to rile him further, so she slipped it off her finger and into the back pocket of her jeans.

Thomas plopped down at the table, his displeasure clear. He took a sip of tea and looked at her, his eyes barely concealing his contempt. "What were you doing last night—getting even?" Not waiting for her to answer, he pushed on. "Because if you were—it isn't funny. It's not enough that you made a public display of yourself—kissing—but you wore a dress that made you look like a floozy."

"Did Blaine say I looked like a floozy?" Stephanie asked, masking her anger.

"No. Blaine said the dress was revealing and cut up the leg. It doesn't matter what he said—you've ruined your reputation and made a complete fool out of me," Thomas lashed out. "Bishop Jon has already called me. He doesn't think we should be friends anymore and asked me to shun you."

She felt a pang of shame. "Shunning is the worst thing that can happen to an Amish, but I'm not Amish. I'm English." And then the words spilled from her like a river. "Daddy knew it would come to this—our cultural differences. That's why he didn't want me to come home when I went away to college. He wanted me to distance myself, and now I know why. We're too different."

"It's true, but we fell in love and you can't deny it. I've hardly slept. I went back to the tree, Steph, where I carved our initials because I can't forget that day."

Stephanie choked back tears. "It was a silly childhood crush. I admit I have feelings for you, but we can never act on them because we want different things out of life."

He twisted the cup in his hands.

"Everything I've done has been for you. I thought that someday you would love me as much as I love you."

"I do love you, Thomas. You've been my rock." He had come every day after her grandmother died and fed her soup when she was depressed and couldn't eat. He'd also fixed the leaks in the roof and built the craft room.

"Well, then—say you're sorry for what you did—repent. And I will forgive you, and Bishop Jon will forgive you."

"I'm not sorry," she said in a firm voice. "I appreciate everything you've done for me, Thomas, but you never said you loved me. And when you told me you'd been with Maddie Yoder, I felt like I wasn't enough. I wracked my brain, trying to figure out what I'd done wrong."

He gently took her hand in his, willing her to look at him. Tears streamed down her face. He wiped them away with his thumb.

"It's too late, Thomas," she said, pulling his hand away. "Richard cares for me deeply, and I've returned his affection."

Sorrow etched his face. "You love me. I feel it." He paused as if trying to work out what to say next, then plunged on. "You've had one date with Richard. That's not long enough to know how you feel about someone. We've had feelings for each other for years."

"It might have only been one date, but it was enough for me. Richard cares about me, and he fits into my life—he's Catholic, and my father likes him."

"Richard could never love you as much as I love you. I've always had our future in mind. I've built something for you for Christmas."

Stephanie swallowed hard. With trepidation, she spoke in a gentle voice, "I wish you hadn't done that, Thomas. I wouldn't feel right accepting a gift."

"My friends had a barn raising for me. I don't want to seem like a braggart, but it's the biggest barn in the county. And I built an apartment in it—for us. I don't have to worry about money anymore," Thomas said, keeping his voice steady. "I hired a marketing manager. His name is Adam; he's made me a rich man. He also helped me design a library for you in the loft and filled it with books. I didn't know what books to buy, but I told Adam all about you, and he ordered books online."

Stephanie could not hide her shock. Speechless, she raised her hand to her forehead, trying to think. If she broke it off with Thomas, they would have an unfinished love story that would haunt her forever. She knew in her heart that she could never follow the stringent Amish rules. Still, he had an emotional hold on her that between them was undeniable, and she didn't want to lose his friendship.

Thomas stood and held out his hand to her. "Whatever you've done, I forgive you. Will you pray with me? Someplace where we can have privacy—your bedroom."

Stephanie dropped her eyes. She hadn't made her bed this morning, and she couldn't remember where she'd undressed. If he saw the black dress, it would only incite anger. He had taken her silence for a 'yes' and took her hand and led her upstairs.

Scarcely breathing, Stephanie dropped to her knees beside the bed, closed her eyes, and brought her hands together in a prayer position. She was feeling like a hypocrite as she scanned the floor for the dress through slits in her eyes.

Thomas prayed fervently, pouring out his heart as if God were present. Her mind was on the dress, and all she heard were bits and pieces as Thomas prayed.

"Stephanie is sorry for her sins and asks your forgiveness; have mercy on her; restore her soul; she denounces the devil and all of his works."

She heaved a sigh of relief when Thomas stopped praying.

He grasped her arm and said, "Pray with all of your heart and ask God to forgive you."

Hiding her dismay, she murmured, "Forgive me, Father, for I have sinned."

"Say it like you mean it," Thomas instructed. "And denounce the devil."

"I denounce the devil and all of his works," she clipped.

"Again, with feeling," he pushed. "You must say it with your heart."

Though she tried, she didn't know how to pray with her heart. "Catholics don't pray like that, Thomas. That's the best I can do."

Suddenly, she felt a rush of wind on her face, and the black book fell from the bed, landing beside her with a thud. They both jumped, and their eyes widened in surprise.

"Is that the book that came from the vintage desk?" Thomas asked, casting a coil of suspicion around it.

"Yes."

Thomas's face paled. "I told you the book is evil. Mother told me there are demons in the book that come out of the book and draw you into the book."

"It's only a book. People cannot come out of books. It's only a fairy tale—there's nothing to be afraid of, Thomas. All fairy tales have evil in them—the big bad wolf ate Little Red Riding Hood's grandmother; Cinderella had an evil stepmother; They locked Rapunzel in a tower. Fairy tales are supposed to be scary."

Thomas cast a stern look. "You don't understand—the black book is Satanic."

"It's a lovely book, handwritten by a quilled pen. I wouldn't part with it for the world."

"I forbid you to read the book," Thomas commanded as he got up off his knees and strode towards the door. He turned and pointed his finger, his look stern. "You're not listening to me, are you? I'll come back with Bishop Jon, and he will tell you the story behind the book. Then, maybe you will believe me."

Stephanie jutted her chin. "Bishop Jon already has a poor opinion of me after last night. I wouldn't feel right."

The door slammed. Thomas was gone.

Stephanie stood at the window and clasped her hand over her heart as she watched Thomas climb into his buggy and snap the reins. Betsy took off at a fast trot. Tormented, a blanket of emotions ran through her. Thomas was a good man and had always been her rock. But things were different now that she had been with Richard.

She busied herself with wrapping a few Christmas gifts, but her mind was on Thomas. She was relieved when he called minutes later.

"Bishop Jon thinks the black book may have caused you to be possessed by demons. He wants to do an exorcism at my barn tomorrow night, if only to quell the rumors. People are talking. They say you're a witch. Maybe Becca said something."

"That's crazy," she said. "I'm not possessed."

He hung up.

Stephanie exhaled. Her thoughts ran rampant. It seemed the Amish believed in evil spirits as much as Catholics. Catholic priests had been doing exorcisms for 2,000 years. A few nightmares and a black book had labeled her a witch. She was sure the word had got out through Bishop Jon.

That night, Stephanie ignored Thomas's warnings, eager to find out more about the girl who had been born with a curse. She picked up the book from the nightstand and opened it, trying to find her place—Joseph had given up his face to Lucifer. She remembered she'd dreamed about the faceless monk after she'd read the chapter. But dreams meant nothing.

She held the black book to her heart. It was a harmless fairy tale. Her grandmother had not given up the book to Bishop Jon, and she wouldn't either.

Ludwig Castle

As Stephanie drifted off to sleep, she had the sensation of falling, as if she were Alice falling down the rabbit hole. Tumbling, she watched the scene unfold before her.

The Feathered Pen dipped the nib in the black ink and magically flew over the pages: *It is time to bring the dark and the light together. Wizard is pleased. Stephanie has joined with the Black Book, the heartbeat of her soul. The spell of the Blushing Rose has fallen away, and Damien is bringing her to Ludwig through her dreams.*

In a trance-like state, Stephanie could feel the wind on her face and could hear the clumping of the horse's hooves as they crossed a drawbridge. She could hear the soldiers talking and knew that not everyone was happy about her arrival.

The gods were angry. A storm raged on that wintry night at Ludwig Castle in the Kingdom of Sirius. High ocean waves roared, and dangerous gales of wind thrashed beneath the jagged cliffs, climbing higher and higher up the cliffs as if trying to reach the girl, the earthling. She was not supposed to be at Ludwig Castle—a dark place. If you listened, you could hear eerie whispers in the wind saying, *Bring her back, bring her back.*

The torrential rains beat against the helmets and armor of the burly guards, but the tough-skinned brutes hardly noticed. Shrieks and shrills filled the air; horses neighed and dogs barked loud as the villagers ran across the cobblestone road to the stables, seeking refuge from the storm.

"It's the girl who caused this," a guard called out to the other. "The seas were calm before she arrived at Ludwig."

"Did ye see her?"

His friend's face reflected awe. "I did. Damien passed by me as he crossed the drawbridge. The girl was sleeping, and she looked like a goddess—young, innocent, and beautiful. Legend says that there's an invisible golden ribbon attached to her back that goes to the heavens."

"What would Damien want with a holy woman?" the guard asked. "He likes his wenches wild and wicked."

The wind carried their voices to Damien. "I will have your heads," he yelled in an angry voice, his dark eyes flashing.

They met his words with grave silence as the giant guards cowered and retreated to the stables. Though twice Damien's size with Goliath's strength, the men were terrified. No one dared cross Damien; he ruled by inciting fear and could be brutal at will. Damien was handsome, and he lived up to his glamorous reputation. He had more wenches than any man in the astral kingdoms.

Stephanie knew she was in a dangerous place and tried to wake up, but only fell deeper into the dark abyss. One thing she knew was that they were talking about her—calling her "the girl." At that moment, Stephanie realized she was "the girl with the golden ribbon," and the dark prince wanted her. A thousand questions ran through her mind before everything went black.

The Dark Tower

The sound of a bolt sliding across metal broke the silence.

Lucifer stood near a large, heavy wooden door with metal bands, his eyes adjusting to the light. A flaming torch on the wall cast an eerie glow over the fevered face of the angelic eighteen-year-old sleeping. He faltered, struck by her beauty, then hurried across the room and folded his long frame onto a wooden chair next to her bedside. He gazed at her, thinking she looked too still. He leaned in to see if she was breathing, then he reached over and touched her smooth hand. She was cool to the touch—too cool.

Other than the four-poster bed, the room was stark and sparse, like a living tomb.

"Wizard," Lucifer stressed the word as a command. In an instant, Wizard materialized, his long, flowing white gown sweeping the floor. He was small in stature, standing only four feet tall, and even with his cone-shaped hat, Lucifer dwarfed him.

Wizard's snowy beard bobbed as he spoke, his voice etched with fear. "I've kept vigil for hours and tried every spell and potion, but she's growing worse." He grimaced when he said, "I've asked Dr. Spade to bleed her."

Dr. Spade strode out from the adjoining sitting room. He wore a black suit with starched white cuffs and a white knotted scarf. His dark eyebrows twitched. "I've brought the leeches," he said as he gestured to a jar filled with black, curling leeches.

Lucifer looked at the girl. "Take the leeches away," he commanded. "She's from the twentieth century and knows nothing of such things. If she wakes up and sees them, she'll be terrified."

Wizard tapped his long, crooked nose and nodded in agreement.

"If I don't bleed her, she may not survive the night," Dr. Spade said. The jar shook as his hand trembled.

Lucifer brushed away a tendril of tawny hair from her face, smitten with her. "The girl cannot die." At that moment, it didn't matter that Wizard had promised her to his brother, Damien, on the day she was born, or that her natural father was a monk whom he had befriended. He wanted her.

Lucifer stroked her cheek with his fingers and whispered, "Awake, my sweet beauty." The words had no sooner left his mouth when he felt a shudder pass over her.

"I think she's coming around," he said with a strange intensity in his dark eyes.

Stephanie groaned aloud. "My head is pounding in pain," she said, wincing. She pulled at her ears. A faint communal thrum sound had settled in them. She opened her eyes, fixed them on the ceiling, and her body went rigid when her eyes roved to the stone, cold, gray walls. She trembled with the grim realization that she was not in her sunny, wallpapered room at Brighton House.

Her voice was weak and hoarse. "God Almighty, where am I?" A flicker of recognition that he was watching her passed over her face. Hoisting herself up from the billowy goose down pillows, she rubbed her temple, blinking as her sleepy green eyes adjusted to the dim light. She froze as Lucifer's dark, penetrating eyes met hers.

Lucifer watched as her body tensed as if she wanted to run, and goosebumps rose on her arms when she threw back the duvet, and dampness hit her, and she sank into the feather bed, seeking warmth.

She shuddered. "Why am I here in this godforsaken place? And where is Damien—my prince charming?"

"Damien, a prince charming?" Lucifer mused. "This isn't a fairy tale, my dear. My brother is dark, as I am. He is the Lord of Ludwig Castle and has gone to his chamber. He is sleeping."

"What is your name?" Stephanie asked as her eyes cast a coil of suspicion around him.

"I am Lucifer, the King of Darkness," he replied. Lucifer was a mirror image of his brother, Prince Damien, but with an undertone of raw power. His eyes burned with an intensity that pierced the soul, and his lips curled in a way that felt like he knew your heart and was mocking it.

She scrutinized him as if she despised him.

"Why are you looking at me like I'm a beast with fire flaring from my nostrils and cinders in my mouth?"

"Because you are the devil," she said. "Everyone hates the devil."

Lucifer did not wince at the blatant insult, but his jaw tightened. "I don't breathe fire, nor do I own a red suit," he said. "Trust me; you are quite safe with me. I am a fallen angel."

"Everyone knows the devil is a liar," she hissed. Her eyes roved over him, scrutinizing his eighteenth-century attire, impeccably dressed in a three-piece suit of waistcoat and breeches. Her eyes left him and wandered around the room, and fixed on the guards. "Am I in bondage?" she asked, pulling the duvet up to her chin as if seeking its protection.

"No," he lied. "There are guards all over the castle."

Her fear and suspicion were clear to everyone. Dr. Spade tried to soothe her. "My dear, you are safe. You have nothing to fear." He noticed she eyed his monocle and looked as if her mind was racing. And then she shifted and lifted the covers, staring at the brass pan with heated rocks.

"My God," she blurted. "What century is this?"

"The eighteenth century." Lucifer took her hand and laid it on the rocks. "We have no electricity, and we must keep you warm."

Stephanie recoiled from his touch and dropped her eyes, refusing to make eye contact. "Don't touch me," she spat. "This can't be happening. It has to be a nightmare."

Lucifer stood beside the bed, burdened with the fact that the girl whom he cared for could not bear the sight of him. "Stephanie," he said as he leaned forward.

He had said her name with such genuine concern, she raised her eyes to his and asked, "How do you know my name?"

"Everyone at Ludwig Castle knows your name," Lucifer said, his nerves stretched to breaking. "We've been waiting to bring you to Ludwig since you were born."

"Well, if you've been waiting for over eighteen years, why aren't you hospitable?" she snapped. "Why am I here in this dark, despicable place? I'm freezing to death."

"The Dark Tower is the safest place in the castle. No one comes here." Her eyes were wary, and he knew she didn't like his answer. He'd been as genteel as possible. He couldn't tell her of the many dangers that awaited her at Ludwig: not yet.

She crossed her arms over her chest. "Where are my clothes?" she asked, looking down at the thin white chemise gown.

"It looks as though she is on the mend," Dr. Spade said.

"I want my clothes," she repeated in a firm voice.

Wizard stroked his snowy white beard, his blue eyes twinkling. "She once had a sweet temperament, but she's grown feisty."

"Why am I being ignored?" she spat. "I want my clothes, and I'm leaving this God-forsaken place."

"She's downright sassy," Dr. Spade said. "Her mouth could get her into trouble with Damien."

"I like her spirit," Lucifer said, raising his brows. "But I fear my brother will not. Never mind about waking him. It might be best to let her calm down. I will take her to my chamber. It's warm there. The fireplaces are roaring. Ring Nettles to bring her food and drink." He swept her up into his arms as if she were a feather.

Her tiny fists beat on Lucifer's hard chest. "Put me down, you uncouth barbarian," she cried out.

Everyone ignored her protests, as if no one heard or cared—except Wizard. "You're shivering, my lady," he said as he snapped his wand. A red velvet cloak magically appeared and wrapped itself snugly around her slight form.

Stephanie's eyes widened in surprise. "How did you do that?"

"Ludwig Castle is a magical place, my dear," the Wizard beamed. "But it's also a dark place. Mind what I say: you can never be alone. Danger lurks in unexpected places, and there are things here that can hurt you…" He stopped mid-sentence because she looked fearful. He paused and wrinkled his crooked nose. "Welcome," he said, waving his wand, sending magical beams of light to her.

"Oh, my goodness," she cried out, her head spinning as her eyes followed the tiny lights whirling all around her.

"Ha," Wizard shouted. "I have found something you like."

"Stop with your blasted magic," Lucifer said as he carried her away. Then he turned his attention to the armored guard and thundered, "Open the door, you idiot."

Lucifer felt her tremble in his arms. He didn't know if it was from fear or cold. He hoped it was cold and not a reaction to him, but given her earlier statements, he assumed she was afraid of him. When he felt her cling to him, his heart rose, but then he remembered he had promised food and warmth. Perhaps that was enticing her.

Wizard floated above her, attempting to amuse her as beams of light danced from his wand. But her eyes seemed to rest on Lucifer's face. His firm jaw twitched as he trudged along, growling at anyone who dared get in his way.

Wizard, undeterred, glided in the air, keeping up with Lucifer's long strides. "When should I wake Damien?" he asked as he poked his wand into Lucifer's broad shoulder.

"There's no need to wake Damien until dawn," Lucifer said. "I would take care of her if she would allow me, but she's haughty and disagreeable. We must fetch Lillian immediately. She will know what to do with the girl. And Nettles must hurry with her food and drink, or I fear…" He stopped mid-sentence because he could feel her shaking. The thought that she might die weighed on his heart. Though his heart was black, there was something about the girl that warmed it.

He held her close and walked through dark, narrow passageways and up spiral staircases. He inhaled. Her scent stirred the beast in him. He tamped his feelings, not wanting to frighten her.

Finally, they reached his chambers in the dark tower. The chamber was elegant. Hunter green draperies hung from tall windows, large paintings and tapestries adorned the walls, and a fire roared in a beautiful marble fireplace.

"It's warm at last," she said with a long sigh.

He watched as her eyes brightened as she took in the luxurious room, impressed by her surroundings.

"It's elegant," she said.

It was the first pleasantry he'd heard come from her mouth. He put her down and asked, "Can you walk, my lady?" He'd thought she might have sea legs.

"Yes," she said, taking a few steps.

"Good. The water closet is there," Lucifer said, pointing toward a door.

She looked perplexed and asked, "I'm not sure. Is there a chambermaid?"

He looked at her as if she were daft and called out, "Lillian, where the blazes are you when I need you?"

Within moments, she heard muffled voices in the distance and the sound of footsteps moving across the room. A lovely young woman appeared, dressed like a peasant, and wearing a white covering over her head, carrying a lamp. "You're awake at last, my lady," she said in a warm voice.

"Take care of her needs," Lucifer said, his concern making him gruff. "She's hungry and cold."

Lillian curtsied. "Of course, Master."

Lucifer turned on his heel and left the room.

"What a relief to see a friendly face," Stephanie stammered, her fear subsiding.

"I'm Lillian, your handmaiden," she answered with a bright smile. "I've been looking after you since you arrived. You've been asleep for over a day. Master has been worried sick and called Dr. Spade to check on you. And he didn't have to bleed you. That's a good thing, don't you think?"

Stephanie's skin crawled as if there were leeches on it. "That's an antiquated practice. Doctors haven't bled patients for centuries."

"Well, it's still done here at Ludwig Castle," Lillian said in a sweet, uplifting voice, "for everything that ails you. How are you feeling, dear?"

"I'm fine," Stephanie lied through clenched teeth. She had a pounding headache but was afraid to tell her, fearing that Dr. Spade would come to bleed her. She was thirsty but perplexed because her grandmother had told her never to drink the water when she was out of the country, and she was in another century.

"I'd like wine," she said, thinking it would be safe to drink and might help her thirst and headache.

Lillian stifled a smile. "I'll ring for the butler, Nettles. He will be happy to bring you whatever you want, my lady."

Stephanie's intuition screamed 'escape.'

Damien

Stephanie's green eyes widened when Damien entered the room with a servant. "At last, you are awake, my lady," Damien said as he crossed the room with authority. He was Lucifer's twin, with a commanding presence, over six feet tall. His handsome face showed concern, and his dark brown eyes flashed, captivating her. Like Lucifer, he wore his black, shiny hair in a middle part, tied back. He dressed like royalty in brocades, a velvet jacket, and white leggings.

"At last, you are awake, my lady," Damien said, as he crossed the room with an air of authority. "Everyone has been worried. You've been asleep for a day and a half," he said. "How are you feeling?"

"I'm very thirsty, and I don't trust the water," she said, unsure of her choice, trying to appear calm. "I'd like to drink out of the bottle if you would open it, please."

The servant, Nettles, stiff demeanor did not bend as he replied in a thick British accent. "It's uncorked and untouched, my lady."

She tipped it up to her lips, savoring the taste and smoothness of the wine, feeling immediate relief from her cinder-dry mouth. "That's better," she said.

Nettles dabbed away a trickle of wine from her lips with a starched napkin and then reached for the bottle. "Perhaps you could drink from the goblet, my lady," he said.

Stephanie pulled the bottle to her bosom and held it tightly, her thirst unquenched. She'd just been snatched off the face of the Earth, and pomp and circumstance meant nothing to her. She stared at Nettles defiantly and took another long swig.

"That will be all, Nettles," Prince Damien said with a dismissive wave of his hand. Mesmerized, he gazed at Stephanie, drinking her in as if he could not get enough of her. Even in her state of disarray, Damien thought her the most beautiful woman he had ever seen. Wisps of tawny hair around her face had loosened, giving her a child-like aspect, and her snake braid hung carelessly over one shoulder. The gown was too large, and one strap fell off her shoulder, revealing ample cleavage.

Nettles eyed Stephanie with distrust. "Shall I take the wine with me, Sire?" he asked.

"No. Leave it. She's not yet accustomed to our ways. She can have whatever she wants—for now."

Stephanie took another long swallow, unperturbed that Nettles stared at her with censure. The wine on an empty stomach wasn't sitting well, and her stomach felt queasy. She sighed and handed the bottle to him.

Nettles grabbed the bottle, his mouth a long, straight line. Her vulnerability and nervousness made her look younger than she was. "Are you hungry, my lady?" he asked with genuine concern, his disapproval warring with sympathy.

At the mention of food, hunger pangs hit her. "I'm starving. I don't want to be a bother. If someone could bring me a robe, I could run down to the kitchen with you and grab a bite—a peanut butter sandwich or a banana—something simple to tide me over until dinner."

Nettles' face turned hard at the idea that she wanted to follow him around like a puppy. "You are not a peasant, my lady," he retorted.

"You are my betrothed, soon to be royalty," Damien interjected. "Surely, you know royalty does not serve themselves."

Her eyes flashed. "I'm not your betrothed. There's been a mistake."

Lillian, the peacemaker, tried to smooth things over. "We don't have such food at Ludwig, my lady. One of us or a guard must always accompany you.

There will *always* be a guard outside your door, as well as a handmaiden."

Stephanie frowned. "Am I a prisoner?"

"No, my lady," Lillian whispered. "The guards are here to keep you safe. There are many passageways, and you could get lost in Ludwig Castle. There are things here that can harm you. It could prove disastrous."

"What *things*?" Stephanie asked, her eyes wide. "Am I in hell? Am I here to atone for my sins? Lucifer is here, so this has to be hell."

"That's preposterous," Damien said. "Lucifer is not saintly, but this is not hell. Men make their own hell and blame their evil deeds on Lucifer."

Stephanie looked skeptical. "How do I know you are speaking the truth?"

"It was your fate to find the black book, and I visited you in your dreams. You knew I would come for you one day."

Stephanie looked dismayed. "That's true, but I thought it was a fairy tale or a dream. But this is unlike any fairy tale I have ever known. You must believe me; I'm not the girl in the black book. I know—because I do not have a golden ribbon attached to me."

"Nonsense, I see it. It's very faint, but it's there. Only those with magical powers can see it. I would know you anywhere. I've been watching you from afar through a crystal ball in the Wizard's den since you were born. You belong to me. Wizard chose you for me at birth, and it's time to begin our courtship. There's nothing to fear." He reached for her hand and brought it to his lips, brushing it softly, desire smoldering in his eyes.

Stephanie blushed.

Sensing her discomfort, Damien tucked her hand under the duvet and turned to Lillian. "Tend to her immediate needs."

"As you wish, my lord," Lillian said, as she turned her attention to Stephanie with an appraising expression. "We must not dally."

Nettles cleared his throat and said, "Dr. Spade requested the chef make a chicken herb soup to strengthen you. I will have a trusted handmaiden bring the soup, hot tea, and crumpets to the chamber—and perhaps a bit of caviar to tide my lady over until dinner is served."

Stephanie's mood lightened at the thought of something familiar. Her grandmother had always made chicken soup when she was ill.

"Take great care with her," Damien said as he turned his attention to Nettles. "She knows nothing of Ludwig or the Kingdom of Sirius. The less said, the better lest she become frightened, and our first evening of courtship would prove disastrous. Tonight, she will stay in my chamber. We will need servants there after dinner and guards."

Lillian glared her disapproval at Damien. "She's very young, sire, and has not yet wed you," she protested. "She's a lady—not like your wenches."

Stephanie drew in a sharp breath. "You have wenches!" She glared at him. "It would be best if you released me, sire, for there will be no happy endings. I will make your life hell."

Damien's eyes were hard and piercing replied, "Have you ever felt the sting of a whip across your backside?"

"You wouldn't dare," she hissed.

His dark eyes flashed with anger. "Don't test me." He turned to Lillian and commanded, "Get her dressed for dinner."

"Come with me," Lillian ordered.

Stephanie shivered, swallowed hard, crossed her arms over her chest, and jumped from the high bed, swaying and feeling discombobulated when her feet hit the rug. Her cheeks turned crimson when she realized that Prince Damien's dark eyes were lingering over her breasts.

Lillian noticed. "Sire, there are rules you must abide by at Ludwig Castle. I would suggest a nice dinner, possibly some music afterward, and your monkey, Snitch, might entertain her with his tambourine."

Damien's tone was bitter. "She's slept through half of our courtship, and though she appears as white as newly fallen snow, she is not. For that reason alone, I will take her to my chamber tonight."

Stephanie found Damien condescending and intrusive. He was treating her as if she had no free will. She looked Damien in the eyes and said, "I have choices. I don't have to obey you."

Damien shot her a disapproving look and said, "You're a woman. You have no rights."

Lillian threw a warm red velvet cloak over Stephanie's shoulders and put her arm around her protectively. "It would be cruel for you to take liberties with her when she has just arrived and is fearful."

Nettles spoke up. "Lillian is right, sire. She's young and the natural daughter of a respected monk. Rumors are spreading throughout Ludwig Castle that the monk, Ochre Eyes, knows of his daughter's presence and is insisting on seeing her. Surely you would not do such a thing to a holy man's daughter, sire."

Damien was brusque as he spoke of her improprieties and declared his intentions. "Though Ochre Eyes is her father, she was born out of wedlock, a bastard, and has no guardian. I care nothing for his incessant pleas to see his daughter. She is here for one reason: our courtship. After *the Feathered Pen* wrote of her indiscretions, I realized I had waited too long. I can wait no longer."

Stephanie turned crimson at Damien's words as she tried to remember her indiscretions. Her hand went to her forehead.

Nettles spoke up. "I must remind you, Sire, that Lucifer has offered my lady protection. Do you not fear reprisal from your brother? The servants have been gossiping. They believe that you have imprisoned my lady behind locked doors with guards because Lucifer is here, not because you fear for her safety. Regardless of the reason, locked doors and guards will not hinder Lucifer. His powers are unlimited. I beg you not to take such liberties lest Lucifer's wrath come down upon us all."

Stephanie's eyes flashed with excitement at the news that Lucifer had offered his protection, and Ochre Eyes was near. Hope sprang. Her thoughts ran rampant. *Lucifer will free me from my curse. And Ochre Eyes will help me.*

Damien's firm jaw twitched. "Lucifer holds a fascination for her—just as I. His presence at Ludwig will not deter my courtship with my beloved."

"Sire," Nettles said. "The gods are angry. The storm raged for the entire night. You have upset The Order of the Universe. She's an earthling and does not belong at Ludwig Castle."

"See to your duties, and do not be concerned with my lady. Wizard will deal with The Order, as always. Everyone knew she would come one day. There is no mystery. And now, our courtship must begin."

Lillian glowered at Damien and pulled Stephanie into a protective embrace, and whisked her away. Stephanie glanced over her shoulder for one more look at the man who both intrigued and frightened her.

Damien's dark eyes met hers and went to her mouth, finding it both innocent and erotic. "Wait," he ordered, closing the distance between them with long strides. He looked down at her and brazenly showed ownership as he pulled her gown off her shoulder, revealing creamy white shoulders, her pert breasts vulnerable.

Stephanie grabbed her gown to pull it up, and their hands touched, evoking sparks of electricity and a river of emotions. *Was it because of the magic?* She fought her feelings. "Don't touch me," she said, her eyes intense.

Damien's fingers, light as a feather, traveled down her shoulder to her fingers. "I'll do as I please, wench. You are my property."

"I am *not* your property," Stephanie spat. "I live in the twentieth century, and I demand that you return me to Earth."

She winced when his hand shackled her wrist in a tight grip. "My lady is haughty," he said in a taunting voice, unyielding. "I am entitled, and our courtship has officially begun. I shall expect you to be agreeable at dinner."

Stephanie tried to draw her hand away, but it felt as if it were in a vise. His strength cowed her, and she held her tongue but tossed her head. Her tawny braid snaked across her back.

Damien smiled a wry smile. He released her wrist, only to show his displeasure by giving her braid a hard tug. "Do something with her hair, Lillian. I want to see it down."

"That hurt," Stephanie huffed. "I shall throw a fit if she touches my hair."

Damien could not hide his amusement. He laughed. "A fit? I should like to see that, my lady." He walked away, laughing, eager for their courtship to begin.

Stephanie's thoughts rambled. She found Damien incredibly attractive, but was astute enough to know that they lived in the Renaissance period, and women had no rights. Prince Damien could do whatever he wanted with her—send her to the gallows, beat her, torture her—and no one could help. She had no male guardian to stop him. Though Ochre Eyes claimed her as his daughter, she was born out of wedlock and was a bastard. They did not consider him her guardian.

A maidservant brought food and drink. Stephanie scarfed down a crumpet, a bowl of soup, and a cup of English tea, nearly choking at what Lillian revealed to her.

"You're younger than I thought you would be. It's only fair that I tell you that Master's wenches are dangerous. They are aware of your arrival and are not pleased. There are rumors they plan to poison you, and for that reason alone, you must stay close to your guards and not wander about."

Her stomach churned, and she set the crumpets and tea aside, no longer hungry. Ludwig Castle was fraught with danger, and once again, her mind sought ways to escape. "I will tell Damien at dinner that I must leave. Surely, he could not expect me to stay under such extraordinary circumstances." But her words fell on deaf ears. Lillian helped her out of her gown and gestured for her to step into the tub of hot water.

When Lillian didn't reply, Stephanie snapped, "For God's sake, say something. Don't you understand? I must leave here immediately. There's been a horrible mistake. I'm not the girl with the golden ribbon."

"You cannot leave until the appointed time," Lillian said in a confidential undertone. "Lucifer is close. He has power over Damien and has offered his protection. Ludwig is not a castle where one lives in a fairy tale, my lady. Danger lurks here. There is a dungeon, and punishments are severe. You must abide by the Master's rules. If you anger him, he could have you flogged or turn you out to tend sheep with the peasants. There is a guard here at Ludwig named Blood Eyes, and he does as he pleases with women cast into the dungeon. I've heard their screams. After Blood Eyes tortures and has his way with them, they go mad."

For all the reading Stephanie had done, it did not prepare her for the barbaric nature of Ludwig Castle. Though Lillian spoke to her as if she were her friend and ally, she trusted no one.

"Do you know what happens to girls from the Village of Wicket and Ludwig Castle who lose their virginity before marriage?" Lillian asked, pouring steaming water from a pitcher into the tub.

"No," Stephanie replied.

"No man will marry a woman who has lost her virginity, and they are forced into prostitution or starve. It's the only way they have to make a living." Lillian sighed. "You are no longer snowy white, and Damien is not obligated to marry you. *The Feathered Pen* writes and has revealed your improprieties. You *are* cursed. It is the lot that you drew at birth. The Feathered Pen writes in the Wizard's den, and a book holds all your secrets. You are in a precarious position and need Lucifer's protection. He is your only hope if you are to get out of here alive."

Stephanie drew in a sharp breath, appalled, not knowing what she had done that had been so horrible.

There seemed to be a sense of urgency, and Lillian constantly looked over her shoulder to make sure they did not hear her. Speaking in a low voice, Lillian told her she once had a sister who had lost her virginity and had jumped from the High Tower because her lover refused to marry her. "She preferred death over a life of prostitution. When I heard of your coming, I knew I had to help you."

"I'm sorry about your sister," Stephanie murmured. "It must have been horrible for you."

Lillian nodded in agreement. "I give you fair warning—Damien is unpredictable. We've formed a coven: Lucifer, Ochre Eyes, Nettles, and several others. There's a young warrior, Magnus, who has come to your aid. Magnus is powerful and very wealthy. His father is King Midas from The Blue Star. It is the richest star in the universe. You must be careful who you trust. There is a sign to watch for to know who is in the coven. It is a hand gesture—a fist with the thumb out. Now we must not talk of this again lest we are heard, and then both of us will be sent to the dungeon for disloyalty."

"A coven?" Stephanie asked. "Are you a witch?"

"I'm not a witch, though there are many in the Village of Wicket. Most live in the countryside," Lillian said. "A coven is a group who are fighting for the same cause."

Stephanie had to know and asked, "Is there a witch in the coven?"

"Yes," Lillian said in a hushed tone. "Her name is Ferret, and she lives deep in the woods in a house that she fashioned out of hollows of trees grown together."

Stephanie's interest piqued. *A witch with magical powers might help.* "Can I go there? I want to meet her."

"No, you cannot. Guards would stop us. Don't ask so many questions. We must hurry. Damien is eager to begin his courtship, though I fear it is more than a courtship that he wants tonight."

Lillian and a handmaiden dressed her in a bouffant, light blue silk gown with a tight bodice and low neckline that exposed more than half of her voluptuous breasts. "This dress is too revealing," Stephanie said as she placed her hand on her bosom. It was the Renaissance, and yet the gown showed more than the black dress that she had worn to the country club Christmas party with Richard Cooper. Feeling exposed, she asked where her clothes were that she had worn when she arrived.

"You won't be wearing those clothes here, my lady," Lillian said. "They are shabby. There are certain ways of dressing and forms of formality that are required. After all, you are not a commoner. You are Damien's betrothed, and you must dress and behave as if you are royalty."

Stephanie drew in a sharp breath. Somehow, she must find a way out, back to Earth, and the sanctity of Brighton House. Her thoughts went to Ochre Eyes, and she felt a sense of urgency to see him.

Lillian Warns of Grave Dangers

It perplexed Stephanie when Lillian laced her dress tightly from the back. "How will I get out of this dress?"

"Damien will assist you in his chambers or call a handmaiden," Lillian said. "I know that escape weighs heavily on your mind, but it is not possible. Until Lucifer intervenes, you must abide by Damien's rules or suffer the consequences. There are ladies in this kingdom who would love to take your place at Damien's side—and in his bed. My advice to you is to stay on his good side. If you lose favor with him, it could be disastrous. You must conduct yourself in a manner befitting your best behavior. Damien has plenty of wenches, but none as young or as beautiful as you. It's you whom he wants."

Lillian's words took Stephanie aback. That she was to bend to a man's wishes and alter her behavior was absurd. She had turned obstinate at the thought and objected when Lillian wanted to take her hair out of the snake braid and brush it. She snapped, "No, you will not. Call in a wench if he wants a woman with her hair down. I will not give him his way."

"Well, you've fussed over every little thing, and there's little time now," Lillian said. "I have some diamond pins and will try to arrange the braid so that you will have some semblance of royalty, though Prince Damien specifically asked for your hair to be down. You're getting me into a lot of trouble with your whims. I swear, I do not know how I am going to manage you. Are you always like this?"

"Yes, I am," Stephanie retorted. "But you needn't worry. I have a day and a half to endure this charade, and then I'm going home."

"Settle yourself, my lady," Lillian said. "I'm giving you fair warning that Master will not tolerate your insolence as I have. He has a dark side that you have yet to see. You do not know the punishments Damien might force you to bear."

"Are you purposely trying to frighten me out of my wits?" Stephanie asked in a haughty tone. "My natural father, Ochre Eyes, is a Benedictine monk and would not lie. He came to my bedside weeks ago and forewarned me of the curse. I thought it was only a dream. He told me I had nothing to fear."

"I have met Ochre Eyes, and he was wrong to tell you that because Wizard placed the curse and only Wizard can dispel it. Though Lucifer is more powerful than Damien, he is not more powerful than Wizard. Damien has Wizard on his side, and together they are unbeatable. And so, you see, my dear, you have everything to fear. Do you not know that this is the Renaissance period? Women have no rights at Ludwig. If you misbehave, Damien will send you to the dungeon and have you flogged. There are torture chambers here and guards who will carry out his orders; Blood Eyes is the worst. And Prince Damien will have his way with you, whether or not you like it. You are *his* property."

Stephanie told herself that whatever she had to do to get out of her predicament, she would do. And foremost, she must talk to Ochre Eyes. He'd told her he had made a deal with Lucifer. She knew, without a doubt, that she would choose freedom over bondage—even if it meant spending three nights with Lucifer. Three nights would be better than a lifetime of torture, which was bound to happen because she could never hold her tongue.

Stephanie's mood had soured when Lillian had laced up her dress too tight, and they had minced words. But she quickly apologized for her sharp tongue, realizing that Lillian had gone out on a limb and gravely endangered herself when she became part of the coven to save her.

"There are rules you must abide by," Lillian said. "You must be agreeable and laugh often. Mind your manners and drink out of the wine goblet, not the bottle. And only eat what Nettles serves you. It is safe."

"What do you mean?" Stephanie asked, puzzled.

"Damien's favorite wench, Bella Franz, may try to poison you. Be wary of any food or wine that might appear out of nowhere."

Snitch

Stephanie was trying to process the information when there was a sharp rap on the door. When Lillian opened it, a little Burmese monkey wearing a red jacket and cap stood with a tambourine in his hand. "What are you doing here, Snitch?" Lillian asked, smiling.

The little brown monkey's shiny black eyes were enormous as he craned his neck to glimpse Stephanie standing in the background. "Master sent me to fetch my lady. It's almost six o'clock," he said. "We must not be late, or Master will be angry, and we will all be in trouble."

"I'll accompany her," Lillian said. "It's not a problem."

"No. I should escort my lady to earn my keep if I expect my ale and nuts tonight. I cleaned the chandeliers earlier, but Master says that now that my lady has arrived, I am required to take on additional duties. The servants say she is lovely, but disagreeable."

Lillian frowned. "The servants have been gossiping—again." She pointed her finger at Snitch. "You must not breathe a word of anything you see or hear regarding my lady, and the guard must go with you."

"Yes, yes," Snitch said. "I understand."

"I know, but you never listen," Lillian fretted. "You're like a rebellious teenager."

She then turned her attention to Stephanie. "Snitch is a favorite of Master's, but you must guard your jewelry. He loves bright and shiny things," Lillian warned. "His name is Snitch for a reason. You will learn soon enough. Mind what I told you. Be on your best behavior. Your escort is here."

Stephanie had been watching from across the room and closed the distance between them. She leaned down and gazed into his snappy brown eyes. "Oh, my goodness, what a little man you are—all dressed up in a fancy red jacket and hat," she mused.

"I'm not a little man, my lady," Snitch said, taking offense. "If you would come with me *now*, it would keep me out of trouble."

Stephanie beamed. "Of course, we can go now. Shall I carry you? I have a cat at home named Boots, and she loves to be held."

"No, you may *not* carry me," Snitch snapped. "I'm a grown monkey, not a cat."

"Let's go," Stephanie said, stifling a smile. "I wouldn't want you to get into trouble with Damien."

"Mind what I told you. Be on your best behavior," Lillian said.

Stephanie started when Lillian grabbed her arm. With a fierce expression, she declared, "Whatever happens, you must stay alive. You must please Damien and do whatever he wants."

Stephanie guessed the outpouring of emotion was because of Lillian's sister's death. Stephanie hugged her and said, "I am not a fool, Lillian. I promise you—we shall see each other again."

Snitch tugged at Stephanie's gown, eager to be going.

It was quite a sight to see Stephanie and Snitch walking down the regal, red-carpeted hallway with magnificent pictures of royalty hanging on the walls. He grasped the hem of her beautiful blue satin dress in one hand and carried the tambourine in the other. She held a folded fan. Lillian had told her to put it away at dinner, but she could open it after dinner. It was to cover a yawn if she became bored with the conversation.

A guard took up the rear. Stephanie knew she would not have many chances to get information. Even though she knew Snitch would object, she stopped short and swept him into her arms. She held him close to her face and whispered, "Do you know Owl and Raven? Do they know I'm here?"

"It's a secret," Snitch said. But he loved sharing secrets and was eager to tell her everything. "Master has locked them away in the library and chained them to their perches. He feared they would come to you. They are unharmed, and I talk to them every day."

"What is it that Damien doesn't want them to tell me?"

"I don't know," Snitch whimpered. "We must go. *The Feathered Pen* writes, and Master will know that I've revealed secrets."

"You must release Owl and Raven. They are my friends," Stephanie murmured with a sense of urgency, fearful of the guard and not knowing if she would have another opportunity to seek help from Owl and Raven.

"Raven is not your friend," Snitch said. "Master sends him to do evil deeds that Owl *will not* do. Could you put me down? We must hurry. If we are late, Master will be angry, and I will not get my ale and nuts tonight."

Before she loosened her hold and dropped him on the red carpet, she said, "You must look at me as a trusted friend. I will get you all the ale and nuts that you want, and I have a jar of bright objects that will one day be yours." She doubted it would take much to gain Snitch's loyalty. He could be a great asset to her in her escape.

When they entered the grand dining room, Damien was standing at the window decorated with red velvet draperies tied back with gold cords. He looked princely, like royalty. She looked past Damien out the window. It was snowing, and she could see tall pines. She would have to find her way to the lower levels to escape. Snitch could show her the way if she won him over.

Snitch glanced at the clock on the mantle and cleared his throat to announce their arrival. "We're right on time, Master."

"Very good, Snitch," Prince Damien said, pleased as his eyes appraised Stephanie. He greeted her by kissing her on the cheek. "You look lovely," he said.

"Thank you, my lord." Stephanie curtsied, just as Lillian had instructed her to do. She had practiced her curtsy for five minutes until Lillian thought it was acceptable, even though she felt like a fool. Stephanie found herself seated at a long, formal dinner table across from the handsome prince and did everything Lillian had instructed: she made polite conversation, let Prince

Damien do most of the talking, laughed when she thought it appropriate, and tried to look interested even when she was bored. She felt that dinner was going well, yet he was looking at her as if something was wrong.

Stephanie watched Damien for signs of disapproval. She observed the slight tightening of the mouth when she discussed the meal with Nettles, the clenching of the fist when she was slow to answer, and the drumming of the fingers when she gave trite responses. Her brooding eyes wandered about while he was speaking, as if she were looking for a means to escape.

"Your manners are despicable," Damien said. "I find you remote and unattainable. You must eat the food and make pleasant conversation. You do not *talk* about food."

By the end of the meal, Stephanie grew agitated, upset that Damien had criticized her—and he wasn't stopping. Nettles looked tight-lipped and pained whenever she asked for more wine and another dish of chocolate mousse. She could not hide her moodiness and displeasure. She didn't know what he expected, and everything she did seemed to be wrong.

Stephanie knew the romantic dinner had not gone as Damien had planned. Nettles had cringed when she struggled to hold the tiny demitasse cup during dessert. When she drank the coffee down in one swallow, he had scolded her. "Sips, my lady, sips."

She could not swoon over Damien as Lilian had encouraged her to do, and she sensed Damien suspected her mood was full of pretense. As the exquisite dinner had come to a close, Stephanie grew uncomfortable as Damien's eyes traveled from her lips to her bosom. Romance was on his mind. She sought to discourage him by engaging in conversation, discussing a wide range of topics. "Is it always winter here? Is there a dragon in the moat? Are there fireplaces in every room?" She rambled, batting her eyelashes.

"No, it is not always winter," Damien replied, closing the distance between them and sitting in a chair next to her. "Yes, there is a dragon in the moat, and there are fireplaces in every room. Do you always talk so much?" He made a bold move, put his hand on hers, and said, "It's time we retired to my chamber, my lady."

She drew away, despising his touch.

He felt her repugnance. "Why do you cringe at my touch?" he asked, his face turning dark.

"It was unexpected, sire," she said, dropping her eyes, careful to keep her tone calm.

"Must I tell you every time I want to touch you? What are you going to do tonight when I remove your dress so that I might see what delights await me under your petticoat?"

She turned crimson and swallowed hard, trying not to offend him, but her words were curt. "A courtship is about getting to know each other. You are not at liberty to do such things."

Damien's dark eyes flashed with anger at her tone. "I own you, wench. Have you forgotten that you are no longer snowy white? There have been many men before me. I've watched you through the crystal ball, and The Feathered Pen has written of your indiscretions."

Stephanie forgot her place and snapped. "It's of no concern to you. I've done nothing wrong. I have every right to be affectionate with my fiancé." She waved her hand in front of his face, showing off her diamond ring as if it would deter him.

Damien grabbed her wrist with manic intensity, pulled the ring off her finger, and tossed it to Snitch, who was sitting in the corner, eavesdropping. "Here's a trinket for you, Snitch. You like bright and shiny."

Stephanie reached out to catch the ring as Damien threw it, but Snitch grabbed it with his nimble fingers and stuck it in his pocket. Snitch shot her a silly, toothy grin, then cowered in the dark corner, crouching down. Stephanie noticed his perked ears. She was sure everyone in the castle would know everything she'd said tonight. And she hoped it would reach Owl. She could see Snitch's hand in his pocket, the ring still warm from her finger, a treasure indeed, for the monkey.

Prince Damien reached across the table, held Stephanie's wrist, and watched her face contort in pain. "A reminder that you must not speak of another man in my presence, for I am very jealous."

Stephanie grimaced in pain and rebuffed Damien's harsh insults and criticism with a resounding, "You're not what I expected, either. You are brutal and condescending and everything I hate! You're hurting me. Ochre Eyes said that you would not harm me."

"I wouldn't hurt you if you would behave," he said, releasing her. "You will soon learn to obey me or suffer the consequences."

Undeterred by Damien's threat, Stephanie hissed, "I demand to see Ochre Eyes."

"Women at Ludwig Castle do not give orders—they take them," he said. "You were once shy, and now I see you in a different light. You are haughty and feisty, not what I had expected."

"Nor are you a prince charming." Stephanie refused to be cowed. "You are arrogant and egotistical. You were polite and nice to me when you were in the book. And you have wenches."

Damien reached over and pulled her near, his lips close to hers. "You're behaving like a wench, and I will treat you like a wench in my chamber," he said in a menacing tone. "In public, for appearance's sake, I will treat you like a lady, though I have serious doubts that you've *ever* been a lady."

"Who are you to make that assumption? You brought me here under pretenses, and I demand that you release me," Stephanie glowered. Thoughts of returning home dominated her mind.

His answer was to bound out of his chair and grab her, showing no mercy as he pushed her down on the table. "Shall I take you now?" he asked, his gaze bold and penetrating. "Or perhaps a flogging might be in order. I'm losing patience. How many stripes will it take to change your fiery temperament?"

It was a sudden movement, and she cried out in surprise. Stephanie looked around. No one was there—not even Nettles. She struggled to sit up on her elbows.

"Don't you dare touch me. I am under Lucifer's protection. Ochre Eyes has made a deal with Lucifer."

A shadow crossed Damien's face. "Are you so frightened of me you would go with Lucifer?" he asked. "Whatever my brother has told Ochre Eyes is a blatant lie." He paused, looking her over, and said, "You might be more trouble than you're worth. Maybe I should let Lucifer have you. You're haughty and disagreeable. I don't know why I even want you."

"Then I should leave," she said, her tone too bright. "You can call one of your wenches to take my place."

"Not so fast," he said, grabbing her wrists and jerking her upright. "I'm not finished with you."

The look on Damien's face told her she was in grave danger, and she blamed herself. She had not heeded Lillian's warnings. She screamed, "Help, help, somebody, please help me!" When nobody came, she crumbled and sobbed.

"Your tears do not move me, wench," Damien said as he cupped her chin and forced her face close to his. "You are mine, and you will fulfill your obligations." He gathered her in his arms and carried her up the winding staircase.

She struggled in his arms, trying to break his grip, but he was too strong. Her mind raced through possibilities to find a way out, but she could come up with nothing. *Where was Lucifer? Lillian had said she was under his protection.*

She glowered at him, her eyes shooting arrows straight into his heart. Damien's look of determination and set jaw further inflamed her. "I hate you, Damien. I hate you," she shrieked.

"Hate me if you must, but I assure you, it will not deter me. You've been free with your favors with others, and for that reason alone, I see no reason to *woo* you."

There were three flights of steps to Damien's chamber, with guards in full armor stationed on each floor. Stephanie knew that even if she screamed, no one would come to her aid.

Prince Damien opened the door of his chamber with one hand and kicked it in the rest of the way with his boot. The only light was a small lamp burning and the flames from the fireplace.

He lowered her to the floor, and she made a bolt for the door, but he was too quick. He grabbed her and unlaced her dress with one hand while holding her struggling body with the other.

"You seem to know what you are doing with those laces," she remarked, tossing him a haughty look over her shoulder.

"This is not my first time to unlace a wench's gown, but it is the first time

I have unlaced the dress of one as beautiful as you. I have feelings for you, though I'm sure you don't believe me."

When he had unlaced her gown, he slipped the dress off her shoulders. It fell in a heap to the floor. He held her against his firm body.

Stephanie recoiled. "Let me go," she demanded, crossing her arms over her nakedness.

"I'll never let you go. In time, you will become accustomed to life here at Ludwig and come to love me as I love you. You're not what I envisioned, but I believe I can mold you into the woman of my dreams. And if not molded, a few stinging lashes will do wonders for your haughty disposition. I'm not ready to give up on you just yet. I have been watching you from afar for years. I was heartbroken when I read what *The Feathered Pen* wrote, and I learned you were engaging in romantic escapades with other men. Do you always trifle with a man's affections?"

"I'm a normal twentieth-century girl trying to live a normal life. Everything was fine before I found the black book, and you appeared."

"You thankless wench. I saved you from heathens when you were under attack. I remember when you were sixteen—innocent—lily-white. You entranced me. Even I could not kiss your sweet lips because Wizard had placed the Seal of the Blushing Rose on you. I watched you through the crystal ball, and you were so beautiful that I wanted to come and snatch you away. I thought the Seal of the Blushing Rose would protect you until I could bring you to Ludwig and marry you. But the Seal fell away, and I'd never felt such pain as when *The Feathered Pen* wrote that you'd been with a man, and then another. You are no longer lily-white, and I no longer have an interest in wooing you."

"There's been a mistake," she said. "I've done nothing."

"The Feathered pen does not lie."

There was only one thing to do. He would not listen to reason. Stephanie pinched herself hard on her arm. "Wake up! Wake up!"

"Damn you," he said. "What do I have to do to make you realize that this is *not* a dream? Must I flog you?"

The look on his face told her he was considering torture. She drew in a sharp breath, watching as his fierce, dark eyes roved all over her body. Standing there exposed, she realized she had been too blunt and attempted to retract.

"Dinner was lovely, and I'm sure you are a fantastic lover. But do you believe I would leave my country estate and well-ordered life in the twentieth century to be under the thumb of a dark prince in the eighteenth century, where women have no rights?"

He grabbed her wrists with one hand and her neck with the other, pulling her in closer, their lips inches apart. "You must accept your place. You are in the eighteenth century, and women will never have rights as long as I rule. It is your duty to serve and please me."

Unwavering, she gazed straight into his dark eyes. "You are a beast. I'm in a dream and I demand to be released. You have no power over me."

Damien ignored her, covering her neck with hot, feathered kisses.

"I can't breathe," she said, gasping for air. Everything went black. She slid to the floor, losing consciousness.

There was a pounding on the door and loud yelling. Damien lay Stephanie on the bed and went to open the door. Lucifer stormed in. Lillian came flying in behind him.

Stephanie lay pale and motionless.

Lucifer's black eyes narrowed. "What have you done to her?"

"Nothing," Damien said. "She fainted."

"The Council has spoken," Lucifer said. "I'm returning her to Earth. The girl is not well."

Leaving Ludwig Castle

~~~

Stephanie's farewell differed significantly from her arrival; solemnity hung in the air as the servants gathered in the magnificent foyer to say goodbye. Damien appeared dark and brooding—his grief so overwhelming that he could not speak. Lillian handed Damien a hooded coat with gray fur that swept to the ground, and he helped Stephanie put it on.

"Are you snug now?" Lillian asked, hugging Stephanie goodbye. Then she whispered ever so softly in her ear, "You will not be alone on your journey; you have an admirer riding at your side. Magnus wants to buy you. It's quite an honor, as his father is King Midas, from the richest star in the universe. They say he would pay any amount of gold for you."

Stephanie froze. "God, no," Stephanie whispered, frantically moving closer to Lillian. "Surely, there are laws. I'm not chattel." Even in the fur coat, she trembled at the thought of being sold.

"There are *no* laws against it," Lillian replied firmly. "It's the eighteenth century. It's common at Ludwig."

She felt little sentiment in her goodbye to Lillian. "Thank you for everything, Lillian," she murmured politely, managing a kiss on the cheek, wanting nothing more than to be gone from the castle.

Nettles stepped forward, his posture stiff. They had given him the unpleasant task of informing Stephanie that, though she was leaving Ludwig, she would return. "I wish you a safe journey, my lady. We shall see you at the masquerade party."

"Masquerade party?" Stephanie asked, her brow knitting.

"Are you not familiar with a masquerade?" Nettles asked. "There will be a feast, and we will introduce you to royalty from other stars in the galaxy, and the townspeople will be there. Everyone has been waiting to meet you."

Stephanie gave a slight smile as her eyes turned to Damien, not wanting to ruffle his feathers.

Snitch tugged at her fur coat. "You must come. I will play my tambourine and dance for you." He clapped his hands.

Stephanie leaned down and took his small hand. "Of course, I will come to the party," she said, squeezing his hand. But it was a lie, and she knew it. Even though Snitch had stolen her heart, she would do everything in her power to avoid returning.

Damien slipped his arms into her coat and pulled her close. "Be safe, my love," he said, kissing her tenderly on the lips.

For a moment, she returned his affection, and her lying green eyes looked at him as if she regretted leaving. Deep down, she hoped it would be their last kiss. It never occurred to her that he had betrayed and deceived her: he had wenches, and he would have her whipped if she didn't behave.

She heard her name and saw Ochre Eyes approaching from the long hall, carrying a silver chalice.

"Daughter," he cried out, "Wizard has made a wine tonic to help you sleep through the rigorous trip. I blessed it myself."

Drinking anything that Wizard concocted frightened her, but she trusted Ochre Eyes and took a long swallow as he had asked. She skewed her face; the wine tasted bitter.

"A little more, my lady," Damien said as he looked on, pleased. Though it was true, the tonic would relax her—she would also lose her memory. He did not want her to remember their altercations and his threats.

Obediently, she took another long swallow. Already, the magic potion had taken effect. It no longer tasted bitter. Her eyes sought Ochre Eyes, wishing they had had more time together so that she might have a greater understanding of the circumstances of her birth.

Ochre Eyes handed the chalice to Nettles. "You are lovely as your mother," he said, stroking her cheek as his eyes roved in the black vacant space that had once held a handsome face.

She hugged him, oblivious to the macabre as she buried her head against the gold cross that hung from his neck, and listened to his heartfelt whispers: "We will see each other again; The Council has ruled that you will live in two worlds; there are things you do not understand."

The Phantom Horseman

There was pounding on the door that swayed the massive chandelier hanging above, and she felt herself being pulled abruptly away. "Enough," Damien said sharply. "Lucifer is here with the King's Army."

"Why do I need the King's Army to accompany me?" Stephanie asked.

"They have to take you through another portal," Damien replied. "It will be easier for you to breathe, but it's dangerous. You need protection."

She sighed, then turned and took Damien's arm as he led her out the massive doors: the wind and the cold bit into her. Atop the cliff, she could hear the waves thrashing against the rocks below, and instinctively knew the gods were angry.

She shrank back when Lucifer appeared like a phantom horseman, wearing a black helmet slit at the mouth and eyes. He frightened her, but he was taking her home. Still, she was unsure and afraid; nothing was for sure at Ludwig Castle. Six Black Knights surrounded Lucifer in full battle attire, also wearing black helmets. It was an unforgettable scene—the phantom horsemen against the backdrop of Ludwig Castle, a force in its own right.

Lucifer wore a full helmet, hiding his contempt and jealousy. "Do not tarry," Lucifer said, raising his voice against the wind as he grew impatient. "The storm is worsening."

Returning to earth was in her mind, but she could no longer read Lucifer's face, and the sight of him in black armor attire made him appear sinister and ominous. Stephanie hung back, afraid of Lucifer's horse, Fury. The beast was mammoth. His wild eyes rolled as he pawed the ground, snorting and tossing his mane, impatient. He was twice the size of Thunder or any other horse that she had ever seen. She couldn't imagine mounting such a creature.

The leader of the Black Knights strode towards her. The warrior was tall and imposing, clad in a black helmet and armor. She breathed a sigh of relief when he took off his black helmet. He was very young and handsome with blonde hair, blue eyes, and beautifully chiseled features. He looked like a Nordic. The chilly wind whipped about, stinging her face and neck. She shivered, both from the cold and fear. She stepped forward, mustering her courage.

He bowed. "I am Magnus, my lady. You must not be afraid. We are not as we appear. We are all young War Hawks."

Stephanie swallowed hard and squared her shoulders. She was determined not to be intimidated by this imposing figure. She thought to herself that she would need a legion of angels to fortify her strength. Her thoughts ran rampant. She had read about the War Hawks in her college world history classes. They had fought in the War of 1812 on Earth. They were young, courageous warriors who thirsted for battle. It seemed strange that they existed here as well.

"We must go if we are to reach the portal before it closes," Magnus said.

"And might I ask, sire, why are you *not* putting up a battle against the Council for her? I would."

"There is no need to battle," Damien said. "She belongs to me. She will return to Ludwig Castle soon."

"If she is yours, I would like to buy her," the young warrior said in a sword-sharp voice. "I will pay any amount of gold for her."

"All the gold in the universe could not buy, my lady," Damien replied. "She is my betrothed."

"My lord, I'm sure you've heard of my father, King Midas. I come from the richest star in the galaxy: The Blue Star. We will pay any amount for the girl."

Lucifer heard him and called out loudly to make himself heard above the wind. "She is not for sale, Magnus. She is the girl with the golden ribbon born of the Light. We are returning her to her home on Earth."

"I thought the girl with the golden ribbon was a legend," Magnus said. He bowed before Stephanie. "I shall ride beside Lucifer and protect you with my life."

Lucifer called out a warning. "Remember who you serve, Magnus."

"My father sent me to serve you," Magnus said, though his voice did not hold enthusiasm.

"Bring her to me, Magnus," Lucifer commanded, sensing Stephanie's fear. "You must not be afraid, my lady. We will not sell you. Not for any amount of gold."

Damien pulled the hood securely over Stephanie's head to shield her from the frigid wind. Her face was barely visible. "Be safe, my love," he said with a worried expression as he handed her over to Magnus.

The young War Hawk swept her up into his arms and whispered, "I will guard you with my life, fair maiden."

"I will be forever indebted to you," she said, no longer afraid of Magnus. "I am afraid to go through the portal."

As they neared Fury, Stephanie could feel the power of the high-spirited warhorse as he flared his nostrils and swished his tail in annoyance.

"Trust me—no harm will come to you," Magnus declared as he lifted her to Lucifer and stepped away. She could feel the power of the high-spirited warhorse as he flared his nostrils and swished his tail in annoyance. She sensed the magnificent warhorse was merely tolerating her. Fury pushed against the rump of the black stallion to show his displeasure.

Magnus mounted his black stallion gracefully and took his place next to Lucifer.

Stephanie felt Lucifer's arm tighten around her waist like a vise, and she felt his strength. The Black Knights lit their torches and surrounded her. She sat tall, astride the magnificent stallion with Lucifer. The torches cast a glow on her face, warming the air. She stopped trembling, feeling safe and warm from Lucifer's emanating heat.

Lucifer pulled her hood aside, and his lips went to her ear as he murmured. "The light and dark together are powerful. Do you feel it as I do?"

Stephanie grappled with her emotions because she had felt a surge of electricity run through her body, but she did not want to admit it to herself or Lucifer. She felt vulnerable when his large hand slid from her waist to her neck. Lucifer was her lifeline. Whatever it took to survive—she would do. The fur coat covered every part of her except her neck, and his hand went there to explore the softness of her smooth skin, if only for a moment. "I'll never let Damien have you," he said in a deep voice as he clutched her fiercely to himself.

Shocked and spellbound by both his invasive touch and his strong words, she could not speak. Though the warriors' helmets hid their faces, she felt their stares.

It was a jolt to her senses when Lucifer gave the command to depart. He took the lead like a streak of lightning. Her eyes were wide. The pounding and thunder of the horses' hooves were both frightening and deafening. It was as if the Black Knights were going into battle with helmets and full armor, with shields, weapons, and flaming torches. His commanding voice said, "Look up into the sky, my darling. It is a sight to behold."

She looked up, the wind stinging her face, and for the first time saw a thread like a golden ribbon that went all the way to the heavens. She was in awe. "Is that my golden ribbon?"

"It is. Now you have proof that you are the girl with the golden ribbon."

"But I thought only those with magic powers could see it," she said, unable to take her eyes off of it, as it waved in the wind.

"You are in a magical place. It won't last long."

And it didn't. The ribbon flew behind the dark clouds, and she lost sight of it. Stephanie stiffened at the noise and rumbling of the horses' hooves pounding against the wooden drawbridge as they crossed over the moat onto land. Lucifer had felt her tense and said in a calm tone, "Sleep, my darling. It will be a long trip."

As the blessed wine took effect, Stephanie felt tremendous relief and thought to herself that her nightmare was over. *I'm leaving this wretched place. I'm going home.* When she floundered between consciousness and unconsciousness and slumped, Lucifer righted her. She tried to open her eyes but couldn't, and finally succumbed to sleep, resting her head against Lucifer's chest, which was covered in armor. He held her protectively, tight to his body. After they had entered the portal, an uninterrupted path to Earth magically opened up to them, and they arrived at Brighton House within the hour. Stephanie, in a deep sleep, was unaware. The elixir had worked well.

She would only remember bits and pieces, believing it was a dream.

Sawyer Rhodes

The sky darkened as menacing storm clouds gathered overhead like a prophecy. The potion had worked perfectly—Stephanie remembered nothing of what happened at Ludwig Castle. Yet she wasn't the same person. Something tougher had solidified in her core, possibly forged in the battle she couldn't recall. This new strength had led her to accept what she once would have refused: the ritual that would cast out what lived inside her. Although she couldn't bring herself to believe it, others did, and that was the only reason she had agreed to the exorcism.

Stephanie nervously gripped the steering wheel to Brier Hill. She blinked when headlights flashed behind her. She peered through the rear-view mirror, debating whether to pull over. It was a black SUV. The occupant of the car seemed insistent as he flashed at her again. After a moment's hesitation, she pulled over. The car stopped behind her, and a man dressed in black, wearing a brimmed black hat, jumped out. He was about 5'10' and moved easily, seemingly unconcerned about the stinging rain.

She rolled down the window a fraction, and he leaned down to eye level. There was an intensity in his gaze when their eyes met. His dark, good looks struck her.

"I'm Thomas's assistant, Sawyer Rhodes. Thomas wants you to leave your car at the lumberyard." He gestured to the building on the hillside.

She tailed him up the hill to the lumberyard with a frown between her brows. He went to the back of the lot and parked, and she followed him. It was raining hard. She jumped out, clicked the lock, and immediately collided with Sawyer, falling into his arms. He was holding an umbrella. He struggled to keep it over her head as he grabbed her around the waist and righted her.

"I'm so sorry," she said, crimson—oblivious to the pouring rain.

He took her elbow and ushered her into his car. "It was my fault."

"You're too kind," she replied. "I wasn't watching where I was going."

They headed out of town and into the country. Stephanie knew Sawyer took his eyes off the road from time to time to gaze at her. She chastised herself when she risked sidelong glances, but couldn't help herself. He had nice lips and a square jaw. He looked relaxed and unhurried. A thousand questions were milling through her mind, and he noticed.

"You must wonder what this is all about," he said in a gentle tone.

"I know what it's about," Stephanie said. "I found a black book, and Thomas and Bishop Jon believe I've come into contact with an evil spirit through the book. Bishop Jon hastened the exorcism to quell the nasty rumors before things got out of hand. At first, it seemed like a good idea, but now I'm having second thoughts."

Sawyer shrugged. "I hate to be the bearer of bad news, but word got out, and there are over a hundred buggies at Thomas's farm and three bishops. All three will conduct the exorcism. The Amish believe you're a witch."

The idea of a hundred people at the exorcism was disturbing, and she peered out the window to take her mind off of what she believed would be the worst night of her life. It was early evening, foggy and raining—everything a gray blur as they sped down the country road.

"Are you nervous?" Sawyer asked.

"What do you think?" Stephanie felt cold as she sank back into the leather seat, folded her arms, and hugged herself. *God help me. I must have been crazy to agree to an exorcism.* Her jitters were growing worse with each passing mile. "How much further do we have to go?"

"Five more miles," Sawyer said. "Thomas told me you've never been to the new barn. There's a big meeting room on the ground floor of the barn, separate from the horses. Thomas holds church there sometimes. That's where the exorcism will be." He paused and asked, "How long has Thomas been courting you?"

"Thomas isn't courting me. We've been friends for years, but…" She paused, not wanting to make her father out to be a bigot. "It's just that…my father would disapprove. Thomas's mother, Emily, is my nanny."

Even in the dim light, she saw a shadow cross his face, and when he spoke, there was more than a bit of criticism in his voice. "I guess a judge wouldn't want his daughter to marry an Amish man—no matter how much money he has."

She darted a sideways glance at him but didn't answer.

The Exorcism

When Sawyer turned onto the gravel drive, Stephanie's eyes widened, astonished at the size of the barn. It was unlike any barn she had ever seen. There were tall, narrow windows at the top, and a glow, as if someone were burning kerosene lamps. She might have thought it looked peaceful and cozy had she not known that an exorcism was about to take place.

Everything seemed to close in on her as she peered out the window. The field was a sea of buggies, a patchwork of horse-drawn carriages stretching as far as the eye could see. The SUV was a stark contrast, its dark exterior standing out amidst the horses and buggies. When the door of the SUV flew open, the man's voice boomed out. "I'm Hombre, the head of the Amish Mafia in Lancaster." He wore a black brimmed hat, and a two-inch scar on his cheek added to the sense of emanating danger.

Stephanie drew back in fear and cringed. Her hand flew over her nose, and she coughed. The smell of horse manure, sweat, and leather, mixed with the faint scent of freshly cut grass, hit her hard. She looked at Sawyer, unsure.

"I'll park the car and catch up," Sawyer said. "Hombre's one of my best friends. You can trust him."

Alarmed to hear Hombre was a member of the Amish Mafia, and Sawyer's best friend—her eyes narrowed, wondering if Sawyer was one of them.

Hombre offered his hand, and she took it because that was the only option.

The rain was coming down in sheets. He threw a raincoat over her head and grabbed her by the arm. She leaned into him and followed along, grateful for the raincoat shrouding her from both the rain and the people.

She could hear the crunching of boots through the gravel and felt the wind cut through her faded blue jeans. Hombre had a tight grip on her arm, but her body trembled more from fear than from the cold. "Get inside, fast," he said with a mixture of command and concern.

The scene was a swirling vortex of tension and mystery, as she realized it was not only an exorcism but a gathering of the Amish Mafia, led by the ominous Hombre. Stephanie's unease and alarm grew with each new revelation. "Shouldn't we wait for Sawyer?" she asked, feeling abandoned. And where was Thomas? Shouldn't he have been waiting for her arrival?

Hombre's answer was to lift the raincoat. She looked up at him. His expression was one of distraction. "My men are all around us: In the rafters, up above the doorways, and behind the altar. They're watching every move—and they're armed. They'll protect you."

"I don't understand why I need protection. I need to explain the situation," she said, peeking out from beneath the raincoat. She gasped. Two men with shotguns at the ready stood before her. Her eyes wide, she trembled, stumbling. Hombre righted her, and she was relieved when the long door of the barn rolled open.

She flinched when a bleary-eyed, unkempt, Amish man dressed all in black leaped out from the shadows.

"Boss," he said, acknowledging Hombre, as his eyes swept over Stephanie, ogling her. "I guess this is what all the fuss is about." And then he disappeared into the shadows.

"He looks pretty rough," Hombre said. "He has had little sleep. His name is Melvin Mast. He's one of my best men."

Her mouth gaped, unable to hide her disappointment. Melvin looked like he couldn't whip his way out of a paper bag. When Hombre removed the raincoat in its entirety and tossed it on a bale of hay, she felt exposed. Lanterns emitted a soft glow in the barn, and it smelled of leather, hay, and horses. Under other circumstances, it would have been comforting.

The Exorcism

Stephanie's mouth went dry at the thought of what she was walking into. The bitter taste of fear lingered on her tongue. She could almost taste the dust in the air, the grit of the dirt, and the harsh, metallic tang of blood. She glanced up at Hombre, disturbed by his rugged appearance. It was the first time she'd had a good look at him. His weathered face and cruel mouth made him look downright dangerous. It was impossible to tell his age, and meeting his gaze gave her a strange feeling in the pit of her stomach. His expression never changed. He was over six ft. tall and loomed over her. His belly bulged over his wide belt. His hand felt heavy on her arm. But it was the gun in his holster that frightened her the most.

She felt Hombre's eyes on her. "You look scared," he said. "You can't let them know you're afraid. There are two hundred Amish here who believe you are a witch. They're here to see demons come out of your body during the exorcism, and some are carrying rifles."

A witch. Demons? His words sent a ripple of fear through her. Her first instinct was to run, and she knew he felt it because he gripped her arm tighter. She felt as if she were in the clutches of a madman. What was Thomas thinking? The men in the Amish Mafia were avengers—notorious for criminal activity, more than cutting off beards. Some were murderers, but there was never enough evidence to convict them. Where was Thomas? It was he who had gotten her into this. A shiver went down her spine.

"This is dangerous," she said, her eyes darting about, looking for a way out. There was a group of Amish by the door, but she didn't see a friendly face in the lot of them and knew no one.

"You're damned if you go through with the exorcism, and you're damned if you don't," Hombre said as he looked her over with scrutiny. "You're beautiful; you could have any man you want. Why did you choose an Amish man? And a deacon to boot. Some people want to believe you're a witch because they don't want an Amish man involved with an English girl."

Dismayed at his frankness, she pulled her arm away, breaking his grip, and rubbed it as if he had hurt her. "Before the accusations, I was an insider to the Amish, but now I expect to be shunned. I don't know what Thomas told you. He isn't courting me, but we're good friends." She paused. "There's a social stigma on both sides. My father disapproves of Thomas."

Hombre's brows knitted. "It was my understanding that Thomas intends to marry you."

She heard loud threatening voices coming from the meeting room: Where's the witch? Bring on the witch, bring on the witch. She felt her chest constrict as her heart thumped against her ribs.

"I doubt your men can protect me, Hombre." She felt like a lamb being led to slaughter. Her shoulders slumped.

Hombre was looking at her in a way that she might have thought threatening had she not known he was there to help. "Get mad," he urged. "Stand up straight and don't look so damned helpless."

She straightened her shoulders and bit her lip. And then Sawyer was at her side, offering his arm, and she slipped her arm through his, relieved. "I can do this," she said under her breath, but when they walked into the vast meeting room, she felt like they had dropped her into a pit of vipers. The taunting stopped, and a hush settled on the room.

Amish people crammed into pews, all dressed in black, with the women wearing their black bonnets—not the traditional white caps with a chin tie, but black ones they reserved for special occasions and events. She had never realized how daunting their black outfits looked, and the number of them overwhelmed her.

The men sat on one side of the room, and the women on the other.

Part of her mind registered that there were also townspeople sitting on benches along the wall. She searched for a friendly face. It was all too much for her to grasp.

She swayed against Hombre's gigantic frame and leaned on him for a moment.

Stephanie edged closer to Sawyer, and he squeezed her hand; his quiet strength calmed her. She squeezed his hand back as she replayed Hombre's words in her mind—reminding herself to stand straighter. Hombre's powerful arm brushed hers. She felt courageous enough to venture a look at the faces of the people who, minutes ago, were behaving as if they wanted to kill her. Now they looked fearful—she could see it in their eyes. One

The Exorcism

woman was shaking as she passed. Men were in cold sweats, even though it was a chilly evening with a breeze. They looked terrified. She realized some believed she was a witch.

And then it happened—the outright hostility and cruelty. "Pinch her," an old woman croaked. A young girl with a malicious expression and pincer fingers ran towards her. Stephanie braced herself.

Hombre swatted the girl with a stinging blow on the arm, sending her reeling and howling in pain. There was a shuffling among the crowd and low murmurings.

Stephanie drew in a sharp breath as Thomas called out from the podium, "Order, order!"

As she stepped up to the podium, Thomas nodded, his gray eyes full of concern. Bishop Jon stepped forward and gestured for her to sit on a wooden bench on the right side of the podium, and Sawyer and Hombre sat down beside her.

For all Thomas' pale countenance, his voice was steady and even when he spoke in High German. Stephanie shifted in her seat, not understanding a word of it. She only understood Pennsylvania Dutch. At that moment, she realized there was a lot about Thomas that she didn't know. He spoke with authority for about half an hour, and the people hung onto his every word.

She stifled a yawn, relieved when Thomas sat down on a bench opposite her. She gave a slight smile, and he lifted his brows, but didn't smile back. Now she wondered what he had said. Suspicion crept into her green eyes. Thomas had always hated it when she gave him 'looks.'

Thomas crossed his arms and stared at Bishop Jon, who was speaking in High German.

Stephanie grew bored by the second, wondering when it would end, until the atmosphere became charged with menace, jolting her out of her boredom.

An older bishop stepped forward, speaking in a loud, angry voice. He stabbed a finger at her. "Are you Stephanie Stratford?"

"Yes," she answered, remaining calm. She recognized him as a bishop from the older sect. Becca had told her stories about him. He had taken liberties with young girls.

"You've got a demon in you, girl." The old man turned to the assembled crowd and said, "Tonight, you will see demons. Prepare yourself with prayer."

Stephanie was losing patience. "There aren't any demons. Your accusations are unfounded." She paused. "This meeting is a waste of everyone's time. I'm going home."

She rose, but the old bishop thrust her back onto the bench, exhorting the congregation, "The witch wants to leave. But I will not let her go anywhere until I have exorcised the demon."

She stared back at him, bold and belligerent. "I'm not intimidated by your snarls and threatening looks. You're acting crazy."

The words had just rolled off her tongue when Thomas reprimanded her. "Stephanie, do not be disrespectful to the bishop. Just answer his questions."

She shot Thomas a stinging look. She had expected more support from him. When she stood, she felt Sawyer's arm push against her and thought better of it.

The old bishop lunged towards her, his features contorted and his eyes wild. "Hear the demon speak. He is bold in his possession of her." He urged the crowd on. "The demons are coming out. They're coming. They're coming." His zealous expression was inciting a fervor in the crowd, heedless of the shotguns pointing from the rafters.

She could hear the shuffling and the unrest among the people. A voice in the crowd cried out, "God help us! A sprinkling of elders glared at her with cold, piercing eyes, and the young men looked at her with unconcealed interest.

Stephanie stiffened. She could feel Thomas's gray eyes fixed on her, his thoughts willing her to maintain control. Her rock was Sawyer. She could feel his body next to her, and it gave her strength and courage.

And then the old bishop was there, leaning down, his bleary eyes peering hard into hers. "Jezebel," his tone ridiculing. "Your green eyes alone tell me you are a witch."

His spittle spewed through the air, and she felt nauseous from the smell of sweat. She had had enough. She sprang up and pushed him back hard. "Get away from me, you dirty old man. You smell like a goat!"

There was a muffled rumbling from the crowd.

He charged at her. "Jezebel, a temptress with one thought on your mind—to entice men. I've heard you have young Thomas in your snares."

In an instant, she felt an unknown force driving her, not of her own will. Squaring her shoulders, she stood tall, her green eyes flashing. Unafraid, she snapped her head and crept toward the old bishop, wagging her finger in his face. "I know who you are, Atlee Hershberger," she said, her voice loud and accusatory. "You disgusting old fool. You have in your snares a young seventeen-year-old girl who cannot fend for herself. Do you not?"

"My wife," he said, "not that it's any of your business. I took her in and gave her a home after her parents died. No one else would have her."

"Ha!" Stephanie screamed in his face, sending Atlee reeling back. "So says you," she cajoled.

Thomas made a feeble move to step forward, and Sawyer blocked him. "Stephanie needs to say what she has to say."

"Thank you, Sawyer," Stephanie said, relieved that he had her back. "You're one of the few men in this room who have any balls at all."

Stephanie squared her shoulders. In a venomous, loathing voice, she lashed out. "I've heard all about you, Atlee Hershberger. You took this poor, innocent girl into your home and enslaved her. You hire her out for housekeeping and keep her money. She cooks and cleans and has sex with you. You should be ashamed; she's a lovely girl. She should have someone her age and not waste her life away with an old coot like you. You're a dirty old man who smells like a goat." Stephanie jutted her chin. "You're a low-down weasel who uses God's name to justify your wrongdoings."

Atlee looked at her with pure hatred.

A trickle of sweat ran down Hombre's face. His men looked down from the rafters, their eyes locked on Atlee. Some chawed Red Man tobacco as they looked down the sights of their shotgun barrel. Some had itchy trigger fingers.

All eyes were on Stephanie; you could have heard a pin drop.

Stephanie cried out in a booming voice. "You have a demon in you, Atlee.

Tell me your name, demon. I command you to tell me your name."

"That's enough," Thomas cried out.

Atlee fell to the floor, but Stephanie didn't stop. She stomped her foot hard next to his head, her eyes flashing. "Say your name, demon," she commanded. "Say it! And then be gone from this man."

She was inches from the old bishop when his face grew dark gray and contorted. His mouth opened and moved all about, and his eyes rolled back in his head. His body convulsed, and he made guttural sounds. Then from deep inside Atlee came a shrieking sound—like a wounded bull elephant crying out in the wild — "I am Legion; I am many."

"A demon's come out of Atlee," a woman screamed.

Stephanie gasped, jolted. She shrank away from the sound of the beast. Her eyes looked at Thomas for help, but he was in shock, his mouth agape. She glared out into the crowd, and they were all terrified, looking at her to do something. And then she heard shotguns cocking. Her thoughts ran rampant. God help me. God help us all. She held up her flat hand to the men in the rafters, hoping to avoid bloodshed. And then, with a driving force within her more powerful than she had ever known—like a hurricane unleashing its fury — she cried out: "Be gone, demons! Be gone."

She felt an arm encircle her waist, and thought it was Thomas come to redeem himself. But it was Sawyer who held her—attempting to shield her—when a whirlwind like a mini-tornado came from Atlee's mouth, rising to the top of the rafters and then out a small window of the barn. The demons were gone.

Atlee's unfocused eyes looked up at the ceiling, and his hand gripped his chest as he babbled something unintelligible in High German.

Stephanie turned and buried her face in Sawyer's chest, unable to look as the terror unfolded around her.

For a moment, the crowd sat dazed. Thomas was staring at Stephanie in disbelief. In moments, like an aftershock of a tsunami, a rumbling spread among the people, growing into a tumultuous wave of stark terror, and an outburst of screams and shouting. The congregation pushed and shoved each other, trying to get out.

The Exorcism

A man cried out, "Atlee Hershberger is dead. The girl has killed Atlee."

Stephanie could hear Thomas' voice, telling everyone to stay calm. "Order! Order!" he cried out. "Calm down, or you'll trample each other."

A shot rang out, and Stephanie felt her knees buckle. Dazed, she felt herself falling in slow motion as Sawyer eased her down to the floor. She saw the faces of Thomas's family in the front row—Emily, Fritz, Mary, Eli — as they sat, paralyzed with fear, their faces frozen in horror.

"They have shot me. Is this how I'm going to die? Isn't anyone going to help me?" She had the grave realization that she didn't feel pain. It didn't hurt to die.

She then felt a muscular body on hers, shielding her. She heard Sawyer's voice, full of emotion, his mouth over her ear, talking low, "Don't make a move, Steph; lie still. Where were you hit? Where is the pain?"

"I don't know," she said in halting breaths, her face pressed into the hard floor, dazed as the sound of the gunshot echoed in her ears.

Hombre leaned over her. "I don't see any blood, Sawyer. One of my men fired a warning shot. I think she's okay. Let's get her out of here."

The room went dark. Someone had doused the lanterns.

Into the abrupt silence that followed, an Amish voice cried out from the crowd. "Stephanie's been shot. I saw her fall."

Maverick Lover

Amidst the mass confusion of shrieks and pushing bodies as the crowd clamored to get out of the barn, Sawyer held her close, carrying her. It was pitch black, but he had the foresight to park by the back door.

Stephanie heard a harried voice come out of the night. "Get out as fast as you can. All hell broke loose." When Sawyer opened the car door, she glimpsed Hombre's form in the dim light as he faded into the darkness.

None too gently, Sawyer deposited her on the front seat. He clambered into the driver's side, saying nothing, and threw the car into gear. She could hear the thud of horses' hooves, brisk commands, and the jangle of harnesses as they left behind the chaos of buggies filled with Amish trying to escape down the narrow lane in front of the barn.

They bumped along what looked like an old cow path with deep ruts, mud flying from the tires. Stephanie felt cold and physically and emotionally drained. She reached for a woolen blanket that was on the back seat. Sawyer saw her shivering, and with one hand on the steering wheel, he helped to spread the blanket over her legs. As they bounced around on the uneven track, their shoulders touched, and Stephanie felt the chemistry between them like an electric shock.

Sawyer cast a quick, curious look at her. "Are you okay?"

Still shivering from shock, she choked. "Sweet Jesus, I thought we were going to meet our Maker. I exorcised a demon out of that dirty old bishop. I saw it, but I still don't believe it. I'm so grateful to you. You saved my life, Sawyer."

Sawyer shook his head. "I can't take any credit. I've never seen a woman with such courage."

Stephanie was relieved when he turned off the bumpy cow path and onto a paved road. They rode in silence until he pulled up next to her SUV. She was still shaking. "I don't think I can drive right now, Sawyer." She knew she should go. There would be gossip if someone saw them together.

She glanced at Sawyer and thought he looked pensive. She clutched his arm. "You risked your life for me. You would have taken a bullet."

"You don't need to thank me," he said. "I did what I had to do." He paused. "I think you need more than a blanket. I turned up the heat, but it didn't seem to help."

She spoke in a halting voice, her teeth chattering. "I saw a movie once where two people were in a plane wreck and used their body heat to keep warm. Would you mind getting in the back seat with me?"

Sawyer had a look of apprehension.

Once settled, Sawyer gathered Stephanie in his arms and rubbed her briskly, down her arms, back, and legs.

"Better?" he asked.

"It's working. I'm getting warmer."

"I've rubbed a lot of horses down, but I've never done this to a woman."

After a while, her teeth weren't chattering, and she wasn't cold.

"You can stop now, Sawyer," she said, not only warm, but he'd ignited a fire inside of her.

He released her, and she drew him back and murmured, "Don't let me go."

When he didn't answer, she closed her eyes, wrapped her arms around him, and buried her head into his neck. And then she felt his warm lips on hers, setting her heart racing as emotions ran rampant throughout her body.

"My God, you're my best friend's girlfriend," Sawyer said in a husky voice. "I shouldn't be doing this."

"It's okay," she said. "Thomas and I have been on the outs. He was with Maddie Yoder when I was away at college. Tonight, did nothing to support me. He stayed with his people. I should have known better than to go there. It's over with Thomas."

She pulled him to her and kissed him again. "You saved my life tonight, Sawyer. I trust you."

Sawyer set his jaw and jerked away. "You're wrong to trust me. I'm a Mennonite horse trader with an eighth-grade education, and you're a rich college girl. The best thing you can do is to get in your car and never look back."

The hard edge to his voice made him seem angry. "Your trouble. I know your father. He was the judge at my trial, and I don't think he would like it if he knew you were alone with me. I'm an accused murderer."

Stephanie drew in a breath in disbelief. It seemed incredulous that the man who had saved her life tonight had taken a life. She'd known no one so bold and blatant about something so heinous. There didn't seem to be anything else to say.

"Don's say anymore," she said, feeling foolish. "I'm sorry. I didn't know."

She opened the car door, bringing a draft of cold air and rain. Already she missed his warmth.

The wind was biting and matched Sawyer's mood when he walked around the car and took her by the arm. He led her to her car. She took one last look at his face. His dark eyes conveyed his feelings for her. And then he made an unexpected, daring move and swept her into his arms. His closeness both frightened and intrigued her. He'd said he was a murderer. But when his warm and wonderful lips came down on hers, it didn't matter.

Fierce gusts of wind threatened to knock them down, but she didn't care. There was something primal and dangerous about Sawyer, but it didn't frighten her—it enticed her. "Sawyer, my God," she said, knowing that she should not act on her desperate need, but could not stop. Feeling reckless, she gestured for him to get into the back seat of her car.

Then he gathered her in his arms, and his mouth went to her ear, and he whispered. "You've got a wild side. I saw it tonight when you went after the old bishop. I've known no one like you."

She didn't deny it. "If I weren't a risk-taker, I wouldn't have gone to the exorcism, and we'd never have met."

Sawyer's voice changed to a husky whisper, "Thomas is an honorable man," he said as his fingers entwined her hair, his lips brushing hers. "I'm afraid my intentions are less than honorable. I'm a rogue, and I'm not the marrying kind. Your father must never know about me. Do you understand what I'm telling you?"

She felt a stab of pain at his blatant honesty and was glad that he could not see the hurt in her face. "I never thought for a minute that you were the marrying kind, Sawyer. Besides, it would never work—a Mennonite and an Englisher." Her heart ached, but she didn't pull away.

As the rain pounded against the windows and the thunder rolled, she threw caution to the wind. Sawyer covered her mouth with his and kissed her. Passion overrode good sense. A soft moan escaped her throat. She was his, and they both knew it. She'd never felt so vulnerable.

It was Sawyer who broke away. "You've ever done this before. I can't."

She sensed that this was the man who was going to break her heart, keep her awake at night, and make her miserable because she could never get him out of her head. He was a bad boy — all they could ever have was fleeting moments.

"I don't know what's going to happen, Sawyer, but I want to see you again."

Sawyer's words were halting. "I have a cabin. It was my grandmother's. No one knows about it. We'll meet there. It's nothing fancy, but it will be a place for us to be alone to talk."

Just as she was about to speak, he closed her mouth with a passionate kiss. She could hardly bring herself to leave. They got out of the car, and Sawyer wiped the rain from her face with his hand and searched her green eyes.

"Tomorrow you might feel differently about me. If you do, chalk it up to a stormy night when two strangers did something crazy. The best thing you could do is forget this ever happened."

"Are you saying you don't want to see me again?"

"I'm saying a girl like you shouldn't get mixed up with a murderer."

He kissed her passionately. "Go," he said. "Before I do something stupid."

She didn't notice the stinging rain. She loved him.

Nor did she see Raven's black silhouette and beady brown eyes as he peered down upon them from a scraggly tree limb, or the black ribbon that hovered dangerously over them like a poisonous snake ready to strike.

The Storm Within

Darkness shrouded the road, the only source of light coming from the faint glow of the headlights. The sleet bounced off the windshield, creating a blurry and distorted view of the road ahead. Trees and fields that lined the road were invisible through the thick veil of rain and sleet.

Stephanie's hands gripped the steering wheel, her knuckles turning white, as she struggled to maintain control of the car on the slick road. Her thoughts, however, were on a rugged and dangerous man with a past as dark as the night itself.

When the car skidded, her stomach lurched. The SUV corrected itself as if guided by an invisible hand. It was a near-miss that could have turned into a catastrophe. Thoughts of Sawyer had distracted her. She worried about the time and whether anyone had noticed her absence. Her parents were attending a party.

Owl's appearance through the blizzard, wings spread wide, brought her unexpected relief as he guided her home. By the time she crossed her threshold forty minutes later, the warmth of home enveloped her, and she made an instinctive sign of the cross. Her phone rang—Thomas' name lighting up the screen—sending a pang of guilt through her chest, his very existence feeling like judgment as heat rushed to her cheeks.

Later, opening the door for Brooks to relieve himself, she winced as sleet pelted her face. The time away had stretched too long; her neglected animals deserved better. A violent gust slammed her against the doorframe, making her scan the yard with narrowed eyes before retreating inside, Brooks already bounding past her. She caught him in the mudroom, towel ready, and dried his coat with quick, firm strokes before he could dash away.

Brooks seemed ravenous when she fed him, which only heightened her guilt for leaving them alone for such a long time. She realized she hadn't eaten in hours, but it was too late to worry about a proper meal. Instead, she made herself a slice of toast with peanut butter and boiled water for a cup of hot tea.

While sipping her tea, she checked her messages and choked when she saw two from her father, clearly missing her. His tone revealed she was in trouble. There were also two messages from Richard, and Thomas had called both the house and her cell, sounding distressed and pleading for her to answer.

Just as she was about to call her father, he rang. "I'm sorry, Daddy. I went to the Amish country for dinner and to do some shopping. I needed thread from the quilt shop."

"That's a weak excuse," he replied in a sharp tone.

"They only have that shade of blue at The Quilt Shop in Berlin. It's robin's egg blue. It might seem trivial to you, but it was important to me."

"Did it occur to you to check the weather before you left? Your mother and I have been worried. Richard's been calling every hour."

"I'll call him," she said, dampening a sponge to wipe away crumbs from the table and placing her cup in the dishwasher. The routine helped soothe her nerves. "I thought he was in New York on a business trip."

"His meetings were over hours ago. He's hung up at the airport. He can't get out because of the blasted storm." He paused. "You weren't with Thomas Shrock, were you?"

"Thomas and I are on the 'outs,' Daddy," she replied, telling a half-lie. "I've got another call coming in. It may be Richard." Another lie. It was Thomas, but she didn't pick up. There was nothing to talk about with Thomas. He had abandoned her at the worst time of her life. If Sawyer hadn't come to her aid, she might have died.

Stephanie's wet hair clings to her face, strands sticking to her cheeks and forehead. Her clothes are soaked and cling to her body, revealing the outline of her curves. She pours the sherry into a glass, the amber liquid glowing in the dim light of the room. The sherry had a warm, sweet taste that eased the chill.

She trudges up the stairs, her feet leaving wet footprints on the wooden steps, and disappears into the bathroom. The warm water pours over her skin, and steam fills the room. She brushes her fingers over the soft flannel fabric of her nightgown before slipping into it. Her body ached, not only from the roughness at the exorcism but also from memories of Sawyer.

The caller ID on the phone reads "Richard," taunting her with a constant reminder of their tumultuous relationship. She answers the call, her face composed into a casual expression.

"Where were you?" he asked, his voice accusatory, harsh, and slurred, adding a layer of tension to an already uncomfortable situation.

"Have you been drinking?" she asked.

"Answer my question, Stephanie. I've been calling every hour, and no one knew where you were. I just talked to your dad, and he said you were in Brier Hill. The stores close at five o'clock. What were you doing?"

She didn't like the way he was grilling her. The conversation was a tangled knot of emotions, with accusatory tones and knitted brows, all fueled by Richard's drinking.

She puzzled over his reaction, but answered his questions with lies. "After I went shopping, I had dinner at the Dutch restaurant. It stays open till eight. I got into some bad weather coming home. Why are you so upset?"

"No one heard from you for hours. And you don't have an excuse. To make matters worse, my flight is delayed because of the bad weather. I worry about you—I miss you. All I want to do is come home and see your pretty face."

She felt a twinge of guilt, but her feelings turned cold when she heard the muffled sound of a woman's voice in the background. Then the line went dead. She stared into the phone. It had sounded as if he were in a lounge. It might have been a cocktail waitress. She guessed that the lines had gone dead because of the storm, but part of her wondered whether he'd hung up because of the woman.

She arranged her plump pillows and settled back with the black book. When she opened the book, a picture of the dark prince appeared. She spoke to the picture as if it were a real person.

"I've had the most horrible night," she said, and then she told him everything about the exorcism as if he were her best friend.

His dark eyes consoled her. Staring into them, she felt sleepy. She yawned and flicked off the bedside lamp.

She dreamed of a wizard. He hovered over her, wearing a white flowing robe with a rope tie. He waved his wand at her. "You must be more responsible," he scolded. "If I hadn't corrected the car, you could have died going over the edge of the embankment."

His blue eyes grew stern. "You cast demons out of a man tonight. Witchcraft is dangerous. The demons could have turned on you."

"I had to defend myself," Stephanie protested. "I believe I have powers."

He waved his wand in her face. "Your powers are strong, but they are dangerous, and you must never use your powers again."

Stephanie smacked his wand away. "Don't tell me what to do."

"You're being subservient," he said in a gruff voice. "And stay away from *that* man. The Feathered Pen writes," he warned. Then he disappeared in a puff of smoke.

By morning, Stephanie had forgotten the dream. She roused from a deep sleep to Thomas' voice, speaking over the answering machine. He sounded desperate, and even though she felt conflicted and bitter because he had abandoned her during the exorcism, she picked up the phone.

"What is it, Thomas?" she asked in an icy tone.

"Adam has contacted a sorceress, and she's coming this morning at ten o'clock to give you a Wiccan blessing."

"I'm fine. There's no need for a sorceress…"

Thomas cut her off. "You were standing next to Atlee when demons flew out. The sorceress will know if they're near you, or God forbid, inside of you."

"I'm fine, Thomas," she said in a condescending voice. "But I'll come because I need to talk to you."

Stephanie hung up the phone. It had been a defining moment when Thomas had not come to her aid, and she needed to tell him it was over.

The Sorceress

Stephanie had mixed emotions when she arrived at Thomas's barn apartment. There was a flood of memories as she passed by the makeshift chapel where, just last night, demons had come flying out of the old bishop.

She trudged up the wooden stairs leading to the apartment. The door stood ajar, and she could hear voices coming from the kitchen. With a deep breath and a determined look on her face, she made her way through the living room and entered the kitchen. Thomas and Adam were sitting at a round table. She drew out a chair and took a seat, her frosty demeanor bringing a chill to the room.

Stephanie glanced at Thomas—emotions unfolding and unfurling at the sight of him. By all appearances, it was almost as if the exorcism had never happened. Thomas sat calmly, dressed neatly but casually in a blue shirt, black pants, and suspenders.

Thomas' eyes were downcast as he spoke. "I know you're upset with me, but I hope you'll find it within your heart to forgive me. Holding a grudge won't help either of us."

"Don't talk to me about forgiveness! You behaved cowardly at the exorcism," she said, her fists clenched. "It was Sawyer who came to my aid... not you."

"I'm not a coward, Stephanie. I was in shock," Thomas said. "There was complete chaos. Demons were flying about, and Atlee Hershberger had a heart attack."

The taste of bitterness lingered on Stephanie's tongue as she recalled the exorcism and the fear that gripped her when caught in the crossfire. "What about me, Thomas? They shot at me, and Sawyer put his life on the line for me and threw himself over me until the shooting stopped. Then he and Hombre got me the hell out of there."

Adam cleared his throat. She looked over at Adam sitting across from her. Papers and drawings were on the table, as if they had been prepared for a meeting. He looked out the window. "The sorceress has arrived. I just saw her pull in the drive. I know you have a lot on your mind, Stephanie, but you might feel differently after you hear what the sorceress has to say."

Stephanie smirked. "Does she have a name?"

"Her name is Mazie Moon," Adam said. "She has a Ph.D. in Religious Studies from Berkley. She's a Wiccan Witch and a direct descendant of a Druid. It took a lot of time to find her, but she's authentic."

Adam went to greet her, and Thomas followed.

Stephanie drew back from the potent smell of pungent herbs and incense when the attractive, slender woman came dashing in—in a flurry. Stephanie frowned and squinted her nose at the woman. Everything about her looked in disarray, including her raven black hair. Stephanie folded her arms.

The woman was somber as she sat down at the round table and gestured for Thomas and Stephanie to join her. Then she turned to Stephanie, clapped her hands hard, and said, "My dear, you are in grave danger."

Stephanie's green eyes narrowed. *What could this charlatan know about her? She looked as nutty as a fruitcake. She should get up and leave right now.* Stephanie's interest piqued when Mazie picked up a drawing from the table and said in a matter-of-fact voice. "You may not realize it, but this barn is a tabernacle. It's constructed in a way to ward off evil spirits."

"A church? This barn is a church?" Stephanie asked.

Mazie's voice took on a mysterious tone. "Adam researched the architecture and went to New England and retrieved the plans from a museum. Thomas had the barn built to plan. There are blessings branded in the wood. Thomas and Adam have enlisted my help and have been working tirelessly to break the curse. I have blessed the quilts on the walls and beds for your protection. Thomas prays special prayers for your soul." She clapped her hands. "This is a holy place. The devil cannot enter here."

Mazie Moon wasn't what Stephanie had expected. This clapping of the hands and the smell of her had given her a headache. Stephanie rubbed her temples. She thought Adam must have noticed her unease, because he asked, "Why are you clapping your hands, Mazie?"

"It's a Shamanic practice. It enforces my magic. It's in the air—it's everywhere. I spread my magic wherever I go."

"That's all very good," Stephanie said, caution making her dubious. "But I don't think you understand. I'm not cursed. The Amish accused me of being a witch."

"Trust me, you are cursed," Mazie Moon said as she reached for Stephanie's hand and made a sweeping gesture with her finger, her pointed, long red nails acting like an artist's pen.

Stephanie's eyes grew wide. There was a mark on her, and the sorceress had only used her finger. "What have you done?" she cried out. "Is this pagan? Are you a witch?"

"Of course, I'm a witch. Otherwise, I would have no powers at all. I'm a Wiccan Witch, and I've given you a blessing. I've marked you with the Star of David."

Before Stephanie knew what was happening, the sorceress had taken her hand and placed Thomas' hand over hers, and said, "I now join Thomas Shrock and Stephanie Anne Stratford in marriage. May God Almighty bless this marriage, the holy of holies; may all the angels in heaven bless this marriage. I now pronounce you man and wife."

Stephanie sat flabbergasted, her mouth agape. Her eyes met Thomas's. "What just happened?"

"We're married," Thomas replied. "She's a priestess."

"Married?" Stephanie hissed. "I don't want to be married. I thought she was giving me a blessing to dispel evil spirits."

Mazie Moon waved a sheet of paper. "The witness must sign," she said, thrusting a pen into Adam's hand.

"It's legal," Mazie chirped. "Adam witnessed the marriage."

"You should be happy," Thomas said. "As your husband, I can spiritually intercede for you. I've taken on your sins."

"That's preposterous. No one can take on another person's sins." Stephanie's green eyes flashed. "I made my mind up before I came here. It's over, Thomas."

"It isn't over. We're married. An Amish man marries for life. The fact of the matter is, you can't marry Richard or anyone else. You're married to me."

Stephanie's eyes widened in disbelief. "Why, Thomas Shrock, you did this on purpose, didn't you?"

Thomas stood tall with a certain satisfaction on his face. "I had to do it, Stephanie. When you're fighting the devil, you do what you have to do."

Stephanie's head was spinning. A tangled web of emotions twisted in the air between them like a knot, filled with anger, regret, and pain.

"No. No. No." Stephanie screamed as she turned and ran out the door. She jumped into her SUV and roared away.

The Golden Goose

Stephanie went straight to Stratford Place. Her heels crossed the threshold, and she yelled out, her voice frantic. "Daddy, where are you? I need to talk to you."

She found him in his study, sitting in his overstuffed chair with his feet propped up on the ottoman, reading the newspaper—the horn-rimmed glasses he was wearing made him look intimidating.

"Shut the door, Stephanie," he said, peering up at her. "News travels fast in Brier Hill County."

As soon as the door closed behind her, she could tell by the look on his face that he knew she'd lied to him last night. It was as if he had been expecting her. She knew he would hammer the truth out of her; he always did. Still, she wasn't sure how much he knew, and she didn't want to dump bad news on him all at once.

He put down the newspaper. "Sit down, Stephanie." His voice was condescending.

She sat down in a chair opposite him and waited. He picked up a tumbler from the stand and took a long swallow of bourbon, then lit a cigar.

The silence was almost more than she could bear. He looked at her and said, "Do you know what you've done?"

"Well, I...,"

Daniel cut her off. "You have stained our family name. It's a mockery. We have sent the wedding invitations out." He grew quiet, his expression stern. "You are so irresponsible—you married Thomas Shrock, an Amish man."

Mustering up all the courage she could manage, she said in a tight voice. "I thought the sorceress was blessing me. The sorceress used magic. It was a mistake; I should never have gone there."

"It sure as hell was," Daniel said, flipping ashes off his cigar into the ashtray.

"I guess you know I was at the exorcism last night."

"Yes. The sheriff called me after I spoke to you. He told me everything. I didn't call you because I knew about the shooting and thought you had been through enough for one night. I was waiting for you to come to me." He chomped down on his cigar. "But you didn't come this morning. You went to Thomas Shrock's."

Stephanie's face was scrunched up in disgust as she caught a whiff of the cigar smoke filling the room. She got up from her seat and started pacing, her movements tense. She stopped at the window, gazing outside with a distant look in her eyes.

"The Amish accused me of being a witch," she said with a bitter edge to her voice. "And the exorcism went the opposite of the way Thomas thought it would. To make a long story short, Thomas betrayed me. He did nothing to defend me when the Amish turned on me. If it weren't for Sawyer Rhodes coming to my aid, they might have killed me."

"I'm grateful to Sawyer. The sheriff gave me a full report. Sawyer is an accused murderer. And the fact of the matter is, you should not have gone to the exorcism," Daniel scolded.

She bit her lip; the mention of Sawyer's name made her heart flutter.

"Why does it surprise you that Thomas stood with his people?" Without waiting for her to answer, he said, "Thomas is an Amish deacon. An Amish person will always take their kind over an English person."

"That's what happened, Daddy."

"It is my understanding that it was his idea to do the exorcism, and he put you in a perilous situation. Now, do you understand why I don't want you in a relationship with him? They almost killed you."

Stephanie folded her arms and stared out the window. "It's all my fault, and if you want the truth, I had a crush on Thomas from the age of fifteen. I was going to come to you and ask if he could court me. But once I got back from college, he told me he'd been with Maddie Yoder. It put a damper on the relationship."

"I knew about it," Daniel said. "Your mother and I thought that the relationship would end when you got older."

"Last night at the exorcism, the truth flashed before me. He had little or no regard for me. He stood with his people and did whatever Bishop Jon told him to do." She paused and dropped her eyes. "Men disillusion me, and I've decided to become a spinster. I cannot marry Richard."

Daniel had that look on his face that he always had right before he was ready to discipline her. His face turned red, and then he glowered.

She put her hands on her hips. "What?" Her hands dropped to her side when he grew even redder.

"You've been making bad choices since Hedy died, and you inherited the estate. I think you have some growing up to do. I've tried to be a good father to you and set a good example. And now you tell me you're going to let one man determine whether you are going to marry. A woman needs a husband. You don't want to be a spinster like Becca, do you?

"It's different, Daddy. I'm wealthy."

"Yes, you are, and there's a lot of old family money at stake. Hedy left you everything she had. You've done nothing to earn it. You have no idea how to manage your money. There are investments, stocks, and bonds. It isn't easy to build an empire. You need Richard. With wise investments, Richard could triple everything you have. You're already the richest woman in the county. "

Stephanie grew bold. "I disagree. I can manage the estate and the investments. I don't need a man to validate who I am. Times have changed. Even Jane Austen chose not to marry. I want a life like hers. Frankly, I see no reason to marry. Men are a lot of trouble."

"You can be so empty-headed, Stephanie. Jane Austen wasn't wealthy. She wrote *Pride and Prejudice* and supported herself and her family. You could live a hundred years on the old money Hedy left you. You don't have to work, but you will because you're a Stratford. Our family has always worked hard and given to the community, and we expect you to do the same. I cannot go to my grave worrying about whether you are well enough to manage the estates." He paused and said, "Since this has happened, I'm questioning your stability. I'm considering putting you on an allowance until you can prove yourself to be stable. My God, it's amazing what you've done in less than twenty-four hours. And you expect me to fix it."

"An allowance!" Stephanie huffed. "If you think for a moment that I'm going to bend to you, I won't. I will fight for what is mine; my inheritance belongs to me."

"It won't be much of a fight with what you've got in your sock and piggy bank," Daniel countered.

Stephanie jutted her chin. "I have money."

Daniel looked her straight in the eye. "You are bluffing. Stop talking nonsense. I suppose you have conjured up another fairy tale character. Maybe a goose that lays golden eggs."

"Yes," Stephanie said. "I have a goose who lays golden eggs — quack, quack, quack."

"You can be so damned annoying, Stephanie. You're an intelligent girl, but somehow you got yourself married to an Amish man today. I'm trying to reason with you, and you're quacking at me like a damned duck."

"You've always told me to be careful what I say because you can't take words back—and so I quacked. I don't want to argue with you, Daddy. And the truth is—I don't want to be married to Thomas. I don't want to be married at all. Besides, he's been with Maddie Yoder. My feelings have changed."

A smile curved at Daniel's lips. "I'm curious. You've had a crush on Thomas since the age of fifteen. What happened? Are you growing out of your childhood crush?"

"He abandoned me during the exorcism, which was the deciding factor." She struck a pose. "But there are other things: getting up at five a.m. to make him breakfast and pack a lunch bucket; having a baby every year; going to bed at eight o'clock every night and having sex whether you want to. An enormous family means everything to an Amish man. And I don't want children."

Daniel smiled. "I'm impressed with your reasoning. I need to increase your allowance."

Stephanie smiled. "Thank you, Daddy. I was going to mention that I went over the budget this month. I had two chairs reupholstered, and the leaky roof on the North side of the house cost more than I thought."

Daniel took a long puff of his cigar. "You're very young to have the responsibilities that I've put on you. I know you've been under a lot of stress, but you were naïve to go to Thomas's."

He flicked his cigar ashes into an ashtray, his expression stern. "I'm afraid Thomas set you up with this so-called marriage. They must have broken every speed limit in the village because they were at the courthouse to file the documents fifteen minutes before you walked in the door. It seemed out of order, and the clerk at the courthouse called me."

"So, you took care of it? I'm not married?"

Daniel frowned. "I'm working on it. They presented a signed legal document to the clerk. There has never been a divorce among the Amish in Brier Hill County."

"I don't know if it means anything, but we did not consummate the marriage."

"I'm sure Richard will be thrilled to hear that," Daniel said in a sarcastic tone. "You're naïve, but you're not stupid."

Daniel stamped out his cigar in the ashtray. "Come to dinner tonight at six o'clock. We've invited the Coopers. Marguerite needs to clear some things with you about the wedding."

"I don't understand," Stephanie said with a pathetic expression. "How can we move forward with the wedding when I'm married to Thomas? Besides, Richard hasn't asked me."

"I'm a judge," he said, standing up and closing the distance between them. He held her at arm's length. "If the sorceress can use magic, so can I. Your mother and I have worked hard to make this town what it is today. I have influence. Sometimes, judges can make paperwork disappear."

Stephanie heaved a sigh of relief. "You can fix it, Daddy? Thank you! I'll never do anything like that again. I promise."

His dark eyes looked stern. "And you need to tell Richard everything."

"He knows?"

"Of course, Richard knows. Everyone in the county knows."

Stephanie looked worried. "How will I ever explain it?"

"Quack, Quack, Quack," Daniel said with a wry smile, his dimples showing, making him look like Clark Gable. Everyone had always said that Daniel looked just like him and was the most handsome man in the county. He turned on his heel and walked out of the room.

"See you at dinner," Stephanie called after him.

"Don't be late," he said. Then he walked back and stood in the doorway, and asked, "Did you buy the Robin's Egg thread?"

Stephanie bit her lip. "I was going to buy it—I was—but..."

"I almost believed that one." He grinned and strode away.

Rather Kiss a Rattlesnake

It was almost seven o'clock. Stephanie's feet hit the wide porch steps hard as she stomped up the steps to the door. The setting sun cast a warm, orange glow on the white-painted columns of Stratford Place. As she opened the screen door, she could hear the distant chatter of her family inside, the clinking of utensils on plates. She caught the screen door before it slammed. Her father hated loud noise. The door closed behind her, and she breathed a sigh of relief.

The entrance hall welcomed Stephanie with its familiar grandeur—crystal prisms catching light from the chandelier above, French herringbone floors gleaming beneath her feet. She paused at a table, bending to inhale the fragrance of tulips and daffodils arranged in a silver vase, before continuing toward the dining room, each step of her heels announcing her arrival.

Richard stepped out of the shadows, champagne flute extended toward her. "To the blushing bride," he said, his mouth twitching at the corners. "Kitchen table nuptials, I hear."

Heat crawled up her neck as she accepted the glass and took a deep gulp. "That's not funny, Richard."

"Oh, come on," he said, eyes glinting. "A ceremony officiated by the neighborhood witch? Was there a cauldron involved? Or perhaps some eye of newt?" His smile vanished. "Don't you think it's time you grew up? It's time you gave up your silly childhood crushes. Put them away with your dolls and storybooks."

Stephanie's face remained void of emotion. Richard's ability to distort the truth was unnerving. "I see you got it all out of my father. That didn't take long." Her eyes scanned him. He has a rugged handsomeness she admires. He is wearing khakis and a pale-yellow shirt, his muscles straining against the fabric. The way he was looking at her was disarming.

"Strange that Thomas would want to marry you," Richard said in an insolent tone. "How many does Thomas want? Eight — ten? That's what the Amish do — make babies."

She knew he would fabricate one if she didn't give him a number. "I would say that he would want six. He's built a large home with several bedrooms."

"Well, maybe he can find a nice little Amish girl to pop them out for him," Richard quipped. "But it will not be you."

"I'm not having children," Stephanie said, lifting her chin. "I'll do what Hedy did—raise money for impoverished children."

Richard's expression darkened. "The family line ends with you, then? You need to have at least one heir, Stephanie."

"Jane Austen managed without."

"Jane Austen wasn't sitting on a fortune. She had no options."

"There are always options," Stephanie said. "She had a proposal from Harris-Bigg-Wither in 1802 when she was visiting friends. She was 26 and Harris was 21. She accepted the proposal because of financial pressures, but withdrew the proposal the next day."

"You aren't Jane Austen—you haven't even written one book," Richard chastised.

"Well, I will—soon," she said.

From the dining room, Marguerite's voice floated in. "Dinner's on the table."

"Coming right along," Richard called back, his vowels stretching like taffy. "Just showing your lovely daughter some affection first."

"Back off, Richard," Stephanie whispered. "I'd rather kiss a rattlesnake."

He hissed and locked his arms around her.

Her body betrayed her with its response to his nearness, even as his words grated against her nerves. She turned away from his approaching lips, her jaw tight.

"A little sweetness wouldn't kill you," he said. "It would certainly make these family gatherings less awkward."

She shoved him away and smoothed her hair. "You are such a beast, Richard," she said with disdain.

They had not heard Daniel come up behind them. "Must we start the evening quibbling?" he said, frowning.

Parker burst in the door carrying a bottle of red wine, in a party mode. "Only the best for tonight."

"There you are, Stephanie Anne," Marsha said, busing Stephanie on the cheek. "I've been leaving messages for you all afternoon. I was going to bring you some flowers from my garden. I wasn't sure if you wanted white or pink chrysanthemums, so I brought both."

"Stephanie has plenty of flowers, Mother," Richard said. "I send her roses every week. Not that she appreciates them. Sometimes, she won't even answer my calls. Not even when I'm sitting in an airport in a blizzard."

Stephanie thought him rude and offensive and ignored his comment with a determined reticence.

Parker reached out and gave her a big hug. "Baby girl, we got a surprise for you."

"Stop it right now, Parker," Marsha scolded. "We're going to tell her after dinner. You never could save a surprise."

"All right, all right," Parker exclaimed, reaching for the wine to uncork. "We'll sweeten the surprise with expensive wine." He uncorked the wine, poured Stephanie a glass, and blurted. "Marsha has booked a Hawaiian cruise for your honeymoon. We're going to cruise the blue Pacific, go to all the islands, and if we're lucky, we'll be grandparents in a few months."

Her mouth agape, Stephanie tried to speak, but the words weren't coming.

Parker mistook her shock for gratitude and hugged her again. "Don't get all emotional, baby girl. You don't need to thank me. We all need to get away from Brier Hill County." His tone changed to serious, and he said, "It will be the best day of my life when I see you and Richard at the altar, tying the knot. I'll have the daughter that I've always wanted."

"You are so sweet, Parker. I love you so much," Stephanie said, kissing him on the cheek. "But Richard and I aren't getting married." And even if she were, she did not relish the idea of having the entire family go on her honeymoon with her. Unable to burst his bubble, she didn't voice her objections.

Parker threw his head back and laughed. "Did I say something? I thought Daniel said you and Richard were getting married."

"Dad, please—why do you always do this?" Richard said.

"It's okay," Stephanie said. "Our fathers get together, have a drink, and start scheming, and that's how things get started. In case you don't know it—that's how you became my date at the Christmas party."

"Don't mind them," Marguerite said, giving her a hug and kiss. "It's no secret they've always wanted you two to get together. I know nothing about what that man is talking about. It's talk, that's all."

"It smells heavenly in here, Marguerite," Stephanie said. "How do you do it?"

Stephanie always wondered how Marguerite made a gourmet dinner at such short notice. But there it was: a tenderloin with small potatoes, asparagus, a Caesar salad, and crescent rolls. The lightly starched white tablecloth, and the centerpiece was yellow daffodils.

Everything was perfect, as usual. They were wealthy and could well afford a cook, but Marguerite took pride in cooking and baking for her family.

"A toast," Parker said as he poured the wine into crystal goblets. "To Richard and Stephanie. Our future. Our family."

The glasses clinked.

"Eat, drink, and be merry," Daniel said. "I'm so thankful for each day of my life that I get to see the two of you together."

"Speaking of eating, I brought dessert," Marsha said. "Your favorite, Stephanie Anne, lemon meringue pie."

"Oh," Marguerite said. "I completely forgot, and I've got a yellow cake with white frosting—you know—because it's unofficial, but I thought it should be memorable."

"What are you talking about?" Stephanie asked, flummoxed. "It's dinner. Lemon meringue pie is my favorite."

"We just want to spoil you tonight, Stephanie Anne. You can have both, can't you?"

"Sure," Stephanie said, wondering what all the mystery was about.

"Dad kind of spoiled the surprise," Richard said. "I've been thinking a lot about it, and well…I've fallen in love with you, Stephanie. Will you marry me?"

Stephanie gasped.

He leaned over and kissed her on the mouth, and when he reached to get something out of his pocket, she stopped him.

"Don't," she cried out. "I cannot do this, Richard. It's all too much after what happened last night at the exorcism." The exorcism had changed her. *What if the sorceress was right*, and *a wizard had cursed her? I*f that were true, she would never have a happy ending. Tears streamed down her cheek at the gruesome thought.

Marsha smiled. "She's overcome with joy," she said, embracing Stephanie. "Oh, sweetheart, don't cry. We're going to be one big, happy family. Forever."

"We've been planning this for several weeks," Daniel said in a gentle voice. "It's unfortunate what happened last night, but I don't think we can let that spoil this beautiful engagement party."

Richard wiped away her tears with a napkin. She bit her lip and didn't answer. It was as if their parents had one common goal, and no matter what happened, they were not to be deterred. Even though they all knew a sorceress had married her and Thomas today, they were moving forward and had even planned their honeymoon. Even though she had not said, 'yes.'

When Richard got down on one knee, she felt like the room was closing in on her. And she said, "Yes."

When Richard slipped the ten-carat ring on her finger, Marsha and Marguerite were so excited that Stephanie didn't want to burst their bubble. The pressure was incredible.

After dinner, they discussed the wedding plans and polished off the wine. Stephanie was in a daze.

"The wedding will be in the gazebo, and I think we will need at least twelve large tents for five hundred people," Marguerite said.

"Do whatever you want," Daniel said. "A girl only gets married once. And I want it to be something Stephanie will remember forever." He took a long swallow of bourbon, enjoying the burn. Then he turned his gaze on Stephanie. "There isn't another man I would give my blessing to. You came to me and asked for my blessing, just like I went to Marguerite's father. You're an honorable man."

Stephanie smiled up at Richard. "When did you do this?"

"I asked him right after the dance at the Country Club. I didn't see any reason to wait until you finished college. I've already made my way. There's plenty of money. As I recall, I took him my financial statement."

Daniel laughed. "You did. And I was more than impressed. But it isn't about the money. Stephanie has her own money. I'm sure you'll gain on her unless she invests soon."

"I can help her with investments," Richard said.

Stephanie swirled her wine. She was independent. It was true; she'd never had a job, but she'd helped her grandmother raise thousands for charity, and that was the life she and her grandmother had planned for her. She was determined to have the life she wanted and not get caught up in Richard's social life, which would take her time away from college and charities. She felt uncomfortable with Richard dabbling with her money.

"You're spending it as fast as you make it, Richard," Parker said, refreshing their drinks.

Stephanie stiffened—*she would keep her money separate and get a prenuptial agreement.*

She breathed easier when Marsha said, "He's joking."

"Richard might have as much money as Stephanie," Marguerite said, "but he'll never have as much land. Can we stop talking about money and get on with the wedding plans?"

Stephanie had not missed the look of surprise that had crossed Richard's face when Marguerite had mentioned the land. Her grandmother had told her never to sell the land. She had bought up every single parcel that had become available. It generated a substantial amount of money. She leased out several hundred acres to farmers for crops. And she sold some lumber.

It surprised Stephanie when Daniel suggested Richard work out of the library at Brighton House tomorrow. "The wedding isn't far off, son. I think you need to put more time into this relationship. You work too much."

"Women are like roses," Parker said. "If you tend to them, care for them, and keep all the weeds away, they'll blossom, and you will enjoy their beauty. If you ignore them, love will die, and they will turn to thorns."

"Flowers turn to the sun," Marsha added with a bright smile.

Stephanie stared at Marguerite, noticing that she had not joined the conversation.

"What's wrong, Marguerite?" Stephanie asked.

Marguerite appeared to be in a daydream, and Daniel noticed. "A penny for your thoughts, Marguerite."

"It's nothing. Coffee, anyone?"

Stephanie wondered if Marguerite was reliving her wedding. Stephanie had seen the wedding pictures. They'd been married at Marguerite's home on a Southern plantation that looked like Tara. There were enormous bunches of magnolias everywhere. Her wedding gown had a long train, and she looked radiant. Her father had looked happy and handsome in his tuxedo. At one time, Marguerite and her father had been in love, but Stephanie remembered Hedy telling her that something had happened between them that changed everything. She wondered if the same thing would happen to her. Would she fall out of love with Richard and have regrets?

Stephanie took a long swallow of wine. *What was love all about, anyway?* Her grandmother once told her that sometimes people who once loved each other fell out of love. When Stephanie asked her how something like that could happen, her grandmother had said, "It's life, darling. We change just like the seasons. One day, we wake up and realize that the person we fell in love with on that lovely summer day isn't the person we thought, and by winter, we realize we're married to a stranger."

Then Hedy shrugged and said, "It's no one's fault." Stephanie knew her grandmother had been happy in both marriages and wasn't talking about herself, so she must have been talking about her father.

Stephanie forced a smile when she realized Marguerite was waiting for an answer. "No coffee for me. It will keep me awake."

Richard squeezed her hand under the table. She squeezed it back. Romance was in the air. Her guard had been up, but she felt it dropping.

"I'll walk you home," Richard said, taking her by the arm and pulling her up. She fell into his arms, and they hugged. At that moment, she was happy.

It felt right that he should go home to Brighton House with her. After all, he was the only man who could measure up to her family's standards and expectations. There was only one thing wrong: she didn't think she loved him.

The Last Seal

Joseph followed Lucifer down the grand hallways and two staircases. He led him to the library in the west wing, one of the many libraries in the castle. Ancient occult books lined the walls, from floor to ceiling—two paneled walls in dark wood held wall sconces that lit the room. Flames from an enormous fireplace warmed the room. He could feel the tension in the air when he walked into the room and felt intimidated by Wizard's scathing blue eyes and Damien's scowl. Joseph did not know what he might have done. Wizard treated him well, though not as well as the royals.

Wizard was in a foul mood. Today, he discovered the monks had placed a protective seal on the girl's heart that he could not break. Wizard sat at the head of the long wooden table, waving his wand as sparks flew in the air. He tapped the table with his wand to show where Joseph was to sit—opposite Damien. Lucifer pulled out a chair and sat next to him. Hemmed in by the most powerful evil-doers in the universe, Joseph sat with a pensive expression.

Wizard pointed a gnarled finger at Joseph. "A monk who delves in the dark can be dangerous. Wasn't it enough that I placed the Seal of the Blushing Rose upon her to preserve her innocence? Why did you deem it necessary to place another seal around her heart?"

Joseph laced his fingers together in front of him. "The monks placed the seal to protect her heart."

Damien's dark eyes flashed. "Speak the truth. You placed the seal to keep Stephanie from finding true love. Only a desperate man would place a seal around his daughter's heart."

Joseph stared straight ahead. He dared not speak the truth. The monks had placed the protective seal so that she would never love Damien — or any man of the Dark.

"You're foolish to believe you can win against me," Wizard tittered. "I am the most powerful wizard in all the kingdoms." He levitated above the table and floated in front of Joseph. "To counter the seal, I will take away Stephanie's memories."

Joseph's face fell. She would be a shell of a woman without her memories. When he spoke, his voice was faint. "I beg of you, Wizard, do not take her memories. What is a heart without memories?"

Wizard stroked his white beard, and his blue eyes grew dark, enraptured with the evil thought. "A heart without memories is an empty soul. Like a dead man walking."

Lucifer spoke up. "Unless your heart is black—like mine. And then a memory means nothing at all."

"Either way, Stephanie will be a shell of a woman unless you unlock the seal, Joseph."

Wizard's mood changed, and his blue eyes twinkled as he sought to gain the answers through trickery and bribery. "I'm a master at solving puzzles, Joseph, but I must admit—this seal has stumped me. Tell me how to break the seal, and I will reward you with a bag of gold and a feast fit for a king tonight."

Joseph sat straight, clutching a rosary in the pocket of his robe to give him strength. The words carried a weight, a significance, as if carved from solid gold and laced with ancient spells. Their meaning swirled around us like a velvety fog, conjuring up a mystical world full of powerful artifacts and deadly intrigue. "I'm sorry. My memory does not serve me well."

The wizard waved his wand, and a Golden Chalice appeared out of thin air, glinting in the candlelight, its intricate designs and jewels sparkling in the dim room.

"You leave me no choice, Joseph. If you cannot remember how to break the seal, Stephanie must drink tainted wine from the Golden Chalice. At the wedding, she will drink wine made from grapes laced with bitters from the tongues of a rare species of frogs. The Golden Chalice shall be blessed one thousand times, and after she drinks the tainted wine, she will lose all memory of her life on earth."

"Who is to place the blessings on the Golden Chalice?" Joseph asked, his stomach churning at the thought of his daughter drinking the tainted wine.

"The one who is most opposed to the marriage," the wizard hissed. "You, Joseph, will place the blessings as punishment for placing the seal around your daughter's heart."

Joseph's yellow eyes roved in the black space, and the tone of his voice grew loud and nervous. "I cannot break the seal placed by thirty monks. It's powerful."

"You're lying!" Damien's voice thundered throughout the castle, echoing off the stone walls. "You will tell us now, or I will cast you into the dungeon, and you will never see your daughter again."

Joseph lifted his head, his roving yellow eyes directed at Damien. "Steel bars cannot hold me. My spirit is greater than cold steel. Do you not understand that I can see my daughter whenever I want? "

"Are you mocking me, Joseph?" Damien asked, his dark eyes ablaze with anger.

"I do not mock you, sire," Joseph said. "I speak the truth."

Damien stood, pointed his finger at Joseph, and looked towards the guards. "Seize him. Throw him in the dungeon. He shall have no straw for a bed, and will sleep on the cold stone floor. Give him nothing but bread and water. When he grows too weak to resist, the rats will gnaw on him, and when he is nothing but skin and bones, take him to the forest, and leave him for the wolves to devour."

The guards strode towards him, but as they were about to grab him, Joseph whirled. It was cyclonic as he levitated above them and said, "A dungeon cannot hold me, and you cannot break my bones. You cannot break me at all because I am a holy man, and own the secrets of the universe."

The Golden Chalice rose and crashed against the fireplace. The booming sound echoed throughout the castle, but the chalice was unbroken.

A hush filled the room.

Wizard stared at the smoke as it rose to the high ceiling. "The monk delves in the dark," he said, squinting his crooked nose with disdain. "His magic is powerful."

"Parlor games," Damien scoffed. "It doesn't matter. Raven has placed the black ribbons that will fill her heart with doubt. Doubt is the destroyer of dreams. She will not love the mortal, and when I bring her here, she will be as white as a new-fallen snow."

"This is not a fairytale, my brother," Lucifer said in a thundering voice. "There are three earthlings all vying for her hand. And though they are not as handsome and charming as we are, they have turned her head. I assure you, a black magical ribbon will not deter them."

Lucifer, holding himself tall, walked with a swagger toward Damien. His dark eyes flashed as he drew his sword. "You are not powerful enough for the girl. I challenge you to a duel. The best man gets the fair maiden."

"I accept the challenge," Damien said, a smile curling at his lips as he drew his sword. "We have not dueled for many months. I think I shall win this time because there is no sand for you to kick in my face."

Wizard levitated between the two. "Two brothers fighting. I won't allow it."

Lucifer scoffed. "This is between my brother and me. Try to stop us, Wizard."

Wizard's eyes blazed red in anger as he sent both swords flying. They rose and crossed, forming the letter X. A sign that meant a *crossroads*. Then the swords crashed into the stone fireplace, sending an echo throughout the castle.

"There will be no more warring against brothers," the Wizard commanded.

"It was wrong to show Wizard your powers," Lucifer chastised, as he stared into the black vacant space in the hooded robe—the large ochre eyes stared back without emotion.

"They were going to throw me in the dungeon—kill me," Joseph said. "I had to do it."

"What's done is done, but you must place the Thousand Blessings on the Golden Chalice. You must play Wizard's game, and you must play it if you want to save your daughter."

Joseph returned to his seat as a spectator watching a game that they forced him to play. "Why? I won't bless a chalice whose sole intent is to harm my daughter."

"You will do it because Bella Franz plans to poison Stephanie. Damien has many wenches, but Bella is his favorite. She's poisoned his other favorites, and the Witch of the Woods has told us that Bella has been to see her for poison mushrooms. We must lock the Golden Chalice up, place it in your care, and recite the Thousand Blessings on it."

"The Witch of the Woods? I have not heard of her."

"Evil surrounds you, Joseph, and I can help you. Don't you see I'm your only ally?"

"It's a game," Wizard said. "Play it. What do you have to lose?"

Damien snickered. "Once you join us, you will realize how weak you are, Joseph."

"I've given you many powers, Joseph, and now you must tell me about the seal," Lucifer said. "What is the seal that you've placed on Stephanie's heart? I promise you. I will not reveal your secrets."

Joseph's fingers twisted around the tie of his robe, the rough fabric rubbing against his skin. He could feel the weight of the occult books in his mind, their knowledge and power held secret in his mind. "They're prayers. That's all."

"Prayers are words, and words are powerful? Don't play games with me," Lucifer said, his voice rising. "Were the words magical rites from an ancient book? Did you use symbols? There are books on the occult in that old monastery, and you've studied them for years. You must know the words."

"There were thirty monks—all praying. How could I know what each monk was praying? It was the last seal we placed before she left the monastery."

Lucifer looked pensive. "Try very hard to remember."

As a servant led Joseph to his room, Joseph looked over his shoulder, trusting no one. He hung his head, his mouth tight. It was true. Words held power, but numbers were also crucial to the occult for the desired outcome. He possessed both, ingrained in his mind, and would tell no one.

The weight of responsibility and danger hung heavy in the air, a tangled web of secrets and power surrounding the Golden Chalice and the seal on Stephanie's heart. The seal that would keep her from love forever.

Joseph alone held the power to unlock the seal. His only choice if he were going to save his daughter was to play their game, but he would never reveal his secrets.

Amulets and Charms

Stephanie knew for certain that something was awry when she and Richard returned to Brighton House. She had gone into her enormous walk-in closet to change into her robe, and she noticed that the big jar filled with the bright and shiny objects was missing.

Stephanie froze and drew in a breath. Someone had been in her closet, standing in the same spot she was, and had gone through all her things.

Richard walked into the bedroom, carrying a bottle of sherry in one hand and two apéritif crystal glasses in the other. Stephanie was pale, standing in front of the fireplace, her white cashmere robe reflecting in the dim light, and the blazing fire added to her paleness. He stopped short and looked at her with a question in his eyes.

"The strangest thing has happened," Stephanie said in a shaky voice. "A jar of amulets and charms is missing from my closet. It's always in the same place."

"Do you think Becca took it?"

"I don't think so. They're things that Raven has brought me throughout the years. They would be meaningless to anyone other than me. Becca's had all the opportunities in the world to take the jar if she wanted it."

"Let's not let that spoil our evening," Richard said, sitting down in the big overstuffed chair in front of the blazing fire, pulling her onto his lap, and cradling her in his arms.

Her eyes swept him. "It's creeping me out a little. Thank God you're here. I don't know what I'd do if I had been alone and discovered this."

"It's only a jar of amulets and trinkets, a petty theft. I don't think it's worth worrying about right now. If she had taken this, I would have been upset," he said as he reached for her hand and gazed at the ring sparkling in the firelight. He kissed her hand.

"I've ever seen such a beautiful ring in my entire life," Stephanie murmured. "John Brighton bought my grandmother exquisite, expensive jewelry, but nothing like this. Where did you find such a magnificent ring?"

"Tiffany's in New York. I knew as soon as I saw it that this was the one. It had to be unique and stunning, like you."

"I love that you're so romantic," Stephanie murmured as she put her arms around him, feeling cared for and loved. The chemistry between them was incredible.

"I was never romantic before you," he said in a husky voice as he smoothed a tendril of her pale blonde hair away from her face. "You've changed a lot about me."

He poured her a glass of sherry, and she sipped it, staring into the embers of the fire, feeling like the luckiest girl in the world. This moment alone was more than she had ever dreamed possible. They had everything that a couple needed for a lifetime of happiness. She snuggled close, breathing in the scent of him, aroused by his masculinity, his hard body, and his chiseled, muscular shoulders. Still, she was unsure that she loved him.

When she met his gaze, he seemed to be deep in thought. "What's wrong?"

"Nothing, but I think it's time you put your fairy tale things away. Even if we find the jar, it should be destroyed. It's not healthy. You don't need charms and amulets and bright objects to remind you of a raven who came to you in your childhood, do you?"

Stephanie snuggled close to Richard and replied, "I don't suppose I need them, but I like them; they're small, intricate, and detailed. Hedy told me that the charms are valuable. They're made of genuine silver. I always thought I would have a bracelet made, but I always thought there would be one more."

"Had I known you liked charms so well, I would have bought you one at Tiffany's. We should start a bracelet about our lives." He gazed into her luminous green eyes. "I suppose I'm jealous. I don't want you to have a bracelet from anyone except me. Not even a raven. I'm curious. What did the charms look like?"

"A rosebud, a wizard, a castle, and even likenesses of Raven and Owl. Each one seemed to have a special meaning, though I don't know what it depicted. I once asked Owl what they meant, and he told me they were magical charms made by a wizard in a faraway place, meant to keep me happy. He told me to gaze upon them, hold them to my heart, and sleep with them under my pillow."

"And did you?" Richard asked.

"Yes, until Emily found them and put them in a jar and sealed the lid so that I could not get into it."

"How did the charms make you feel?"

"Special and happy. I was young and impressionable, and when I told my stories about the handsome prince that I was going to marry one day, everyone would smile and say that I had an active imagination."

"Did Raven ever bring you other things besides the charms?"

"Yes, bright and shiny objects and ribbons for my hair. Hedy called them 'junk' but let me keep them. And when I wore a ribbon in my hair that Raven brought me, I thought I could fly." Stephanie's voice turned somber as she remembered that tragic day.

"I had a black ribbon in my hair the day that Old Paint died. Raven had dropped the ribbon in my path. This ribbon felt a little different from the other things he had brought to me. And when I rode Old Paint that day, I somehow thought that we could both fly and that he could do the jumps that I wanted him to do. But he couldn't. He was too old and died right under me."

"Did you tell anyone about the ribbon?"

"I told my grandmother, and she told me that a ribbon could not make me fly." She burned the ribbon. "I was aghast when I watched my magic ribbon go up in smoke."

"Let's not talk about it anymore, darling," Richard said. "The next time

I go to New York, I'll buy you a charm bracelet. It will be about our life, not some imaginary place that exists only in your mind. We'll have a new beginning."

"A new beginning? I'm happy with my life, Richard. It's just that I've had some unusual things happen during the past few weeks. I think you should know that I'm old-fashioned. My family is about tradition, and we treasure the past."

"My family treasures the past, too, but we don't have amulets and magic in our lives. Once we're engaged, I would expect you to give all that up."

"I'm not sure I can do that, Richard," she protested. "It's part of who I am."

Richard frowned. "We'll talk about it later. I have an early get-up. I have to go to New York on business."

He kissed her goodnight and left.

When she put Brooks out to do his business, she realized Richard hadn't gone far. His voice was carrying to her as clearly as if he were in the same room. "I will explain everything tomorrow, honey. We'll go to dinner. It's a long story. It's complicated," he said.

Stephanie rationalized that he was breaking up with an old flame, so she shouldn't worry. But why would he call her 'honey' if he were breaking up with her?

As she drifted off to sleep, she felt someone in a faraway place was watching her. She told herself it was only her imagination. Stephanie dreamed a disturbing dream in which she was being held in bondage. She ran her hand up the concrete wall, and it was cold. There were bars and a tiny opening, and when she looked out, she saw Richard's face looking back; his eyes were hard.

He was her jailer.

She woke herself up screaming. After getting up and having a glass of milk, she read for a while, then fell back to sleep, only to have another dream.

Thomas was in a dream, and they were in the forest at the tree where he had carved their initials. "You're mine," Thomas said. "We're married."

Then she saw rocks being flung at her by the Amish, and she ran through the forest. There was a log cabin in the clearing, and she ran there for cover.

The door opened, and she fell into the man's arms — Sawyer.

A man's voice thundered. "Daughter, this man is your true love."

The next morning, she tried to make sense of the dream, but couldn't. She made herself a cup of green tea, as she wasn't feeling hungry. Her mind was on the dream.

The ringing of the phone brought her out of her daydream.

"I'm at the airport and have a few minutes before the plane leaves," Richard said. "I feel guilty for leaving you, but it's a big case."

Stephanie tunneled her fingers through her tousled hair. "It's okay. I just got up."

"What are you going to do today?"

"I'm not sure. There's always something to do in this big house. I'm still cleaning out drawers and closets."

"Are you going out?"

"I'm not sure."

"After what happened the other night, I'm not sure you should go anywhere at all. I get nervous when I don't know where you are."

"You're just like my father," she said.

"I've been thinking, and we need to talk when I get back about the amulets, dolls, and the fairy tales Hedy used to tell you. It isn't normal, honey. You might need to see a psychiatrist. Sometimes your imagination runs away from you."

It was the first time he'd said anything like that to her, and her demeanor turned sullen and cold. He'd been sexy and charming last night. And now he's saying she might need a psychiatrist. Her demeanor turned sullen and cold as she remembered he would meet with a woman, someone he'd called 'honey.'

"Goodbye, Richard," she said in a high-pitched voice. "Have a safe trip."

She slammed down the phone, her mind on her lost amulets and charms.

Then she went outside and to the great oak tree where Raven often perched.

"Raven," she cried out in a mournful voice. "My amulets and charms are gone. You must help me find them."

She heard a rustle in the trees, then caught sight of the black bird taking flight. Thank God he'd heard her. She breathed a sigh of relief as she watched Raven soar through the blue sky. He would find her treasures; she was sure of it.

She went back into the house and put the teapot on to boil. Then something caught her eye under a chair. Reaching down, she picked up a black ribbon, thinking it must have trailed out of her sewing box when she'd sewn on a button for Richard.

Doubt filled her mind. Doubt that marrying Richard would give her a fairy tale ending. *And who was that woman he'd been talking to on the phone last night? He'd called her honey.*

Black Ribbons

Stephanie was at odds and angry with Daniel. He had done the despicable—he'd left for Charleston. His departure had been sudden, and he hadn't said goodbye. Becca had broken the news to her that morning when she woke up. Stephanie had been livid—ranting and raving. When she wouldn't stop, Becca blurted out the truth, that Daniel had a heart problem. Marguerite trusted only her old family doctors, and she had insisted that they leave for Charleston right away to see a heart specialist.

"He should have told me he was going," Stephanie lashed out.

Becca wrung her hands on her white apron. "Daniel didn't want to worry you. He didn't want you to know he'd been ill."

Anger turned to guilt, and Stephanie blamed herself for her father's illness. She promised herself that she would not ruffle the waters. She was glad when Becca went home so she could be alone and sort out her thoughts.

It was late afternoon when Stephanie—feeling restless, bundled up in layers of sweaters and a heavy coat—threw a red wool scarf around her neck and slipped into an old pair of black, lined rubber boots. She stuck her cell phone in her pocket and set out with Brooks to get some fresh air and exercise. She would walk to the family cemetery and tend the graves.

They got a late start. It was late afternoon, cold, and overcast, and over a mile to the family plot. Brooks ran ahead, and when a rabbit jumped out of the bushes, he bounded off after it.

"Come back, Brooks," Stephanie scolded, her breath frigid as she hurried down the cobblestone drive. "This is not the time to chase rabbits."

Stephanie stopped at the wide gate that separated the two vast country estates and gazed up at Stratford Place, high on the hill. It looked dark and gloomy, and its shadow loomed over the countryside. Marguerite always lit candles on cloudy days, but she was in Charleston. It was too quiet, and she had an eerie feeling, as if someone were watching her. She peered at the windows at Stratford Place, squinting, wondering if someone was watching her from behind the white lace curtains, but they were all in place. *It's only my imagination.*

Her eyes traced the cobblestone lane down the hill to the big, wrought-iron gate. It was closed, but not locked. Bradley would lock it when he came home tonight. Last, her eyes scanned the estate in its entirety, enclosed by white fencing that went on for miles.

She sighed in relief. "Everything is fine, Brooks. I don't know why I have the heebie-jeebies."

Brooks whined, and Stephanie walked on with a purpose. She wanted to talk to her dead ancestors. They were her family and would understand. When Hedy was alive, they had talked every day about everything imaginable.

She stepped up her pace, eager to reach the cemetery. After Hedy died, she talked to Becca but never told her anything of importance. Becca was close-minded and set in her ways. She had gone to the eighth grade and had never ventured beyond the next county when she visited a cousin. She would speak in parables or repeat what she'd heard other people say. Her answers were always concise: *A tiger's stripes never change; the grass is always greener on the other side of the fence; that frown is going to freeze on your face; don't cry over spilled milk, and the early bird gets the worm.*

Stephanie passed by the orchard, now barren of fruit, and a big hickory tree where she had gathered nuts in the fall. There was a movement in her peripheral vision. She squinted as she stood motionless, staring hard at the big pond. She made a split-second decision to pursue the intruder and walked over an embankment to the pond where she swam on sweltering summer days. The pond looked stark with pieces of ice, and the rock where she sunned herself looked slippery with a thin glaze of ice.

There it was again, a movement. It had been ever so slight, but something had moved. Stephanie quickened her pace, intent on finding the intruder, her eyes scanning the pond. It was then that she noticed a bunch of sticks piled high at the edge of the bank. And then she saw it: a muskrat building a den. A faint smile came to her lips. She stood motionless, not making a sound, hoping to blend in with nature. Surprisingly, Brooks followed suit.

It was one of those rare moments in nature that she loved when she came upon something unexpected. Her smile grew broader as she thought of Thomas and the chittering sound that he made to amuse her. She missed him.

She ventured closer down the sloping ground toward the pond, hoping to see other muskrats, maybe their offspring. She pushed entangled tendrils from a gnarled, giant oak tree out of her way and looked up.

It was then that she saw him—Raven—perched high on a limb of the oak tree. Her mood changed from adventurous to uneasy. His small, beady eyes watched her every move. Was he spying? A shiver went down her spine. Thinking about it too much could drive her crazy. She ignored Raven, hoping he would go away.

Brooks took her gloved hand in his wet mouth and tugged, sensing something was wrong.

"Okay, Brooks," she said in a whisper, not wanting to disturb the muskrat. "I'm going."

She trudged up the bank with Brooks leading the way. Seeing the muskrat had reminded her of Thomas and set off a yearning inside of her. She struggled within herself to make sense of all that had happened. *If only I had waited*, she thought to herself, *and not gotten involved with Richard. I love Thomas. I should have, I should have...*

Twigs snapped under her boots as she trampled through some dense brush to get back to the path. She looked over her shoulder. The muskrat had stopped working on the den and was staring at her, his beady, black feral eyes penetrating, his tiny ears perked. She met his gaze and stood still, enjoying the silent communication with the small animal. A flock of geese honking flew overhead in a V formation and broke the spell. Still, the muskrat stood motionless. She breathed a sigh of relief that the geese had not landed in the pond and interrupted the muskrat's progress.

The sky had turned from light dusk to dark gray. Stephanie broke into a half jog, slowed by her heavy waterproof boots. She was glad to be back on the path, but was very much aware that Raven was circling above maliciously. She heard the flutter of his wings but didn't bother to look, so she didn't see the black ribbon that he clenched in his beak, trailing along behind him. The storm was moving fast, and she forged on toward the cemetery. The muskrat had distracted her, and she'd lost track of time.

Stephanie's thoughts rambled. Doubt grew stronger. Who was the woman Richard was on the phone with last night? She trudged along, unable to let it go—dredging up bits and pieces of what she'd heard. Was she an attorney? Or maybe she was a woman he'd known for years—someone he'd dated when he was in the NFL. Was she a client? A rich woman who fell in love with him during a trial. Or a loose woman he'd met who gave away sexual favors to be with a high-ranking man. What did he mean when he said, "It's complicated?"

"It won't be for long, Richard," she said, speaking into the wind. "Because I'm breaking our engagement." It was all-consuming, and she was ready to call it quits. And then she thought about the ramifications of what could happen to her father if she were to break up with Richard. He could have a setback. *No. No. I can't do it with Daddy having a heart problem. I'm overthinking this. I don't know who the woman is—maybe she's a difficult client.*

It was difficult because Richard could be charming and loving, but she saw a side of him that frightened her. He was manipulative and controlling—and he could be cheating on her at this very minute.

She felt so alone.

Gargoyles and Tombstones

Stephanie froze when a crow cawed. She had finally reached the entrance to the old family cemetery, where two large gargoyles stood guard. Her slight frame pushed hard against the old iron gate, relieved when it finally creaked open, but she jumped when it closed on its own with a loud clang. She stood, gazing at the old tombstones, but the comforting feeling that she'd hoped for wasn't there. She felt just as alone and lost in the graveyard with her ancestors as she had at Brighton House.

Storm clouds hovered above. She told herself that she must hurry. She ran to the freshest grave and touched the tombstone lovingly, then brushed away leaves and poured out her troubles.

"Grandmother, my whole life is in a shamble. The Amish have shunned me. Shunning is brutal and cruel. People who once loved me won't even look at me when I pass by them on the street. It's like I'm invisible to them. There was an exorcism, and I saw demons come out of an old bishop. It was horrible."

She closed her eyes and said a prayer, just like she always did when she'd visited the graves with her grandmother. "Hail Mary, full of grace, pray for us sinners, now and at the hour of our death."

The ground felt cold, and she felt a movement near her hand. She thought it was a twig, but when she looked, it moved. It was long and black, crawling up her arm. A scream stuck in her throat, and she flung her arm this way and that way, trying to cast off the snake. She shouted into the dark sky.

"Help, help!"

The harsh whistling wind seemed to answer her, calling out, *Stephanie, Stephanie.*

Raven dove and snatched the snake in its beak.

Stephanie watched, unsure if it was a snake or a black ribbon as it trailed away, the wind whipping it about. Instead of being grateful, Stephanie cursed the bird. "You despicable bird, get off my land! You're evil and I know it." Exhausted, her voice faltered and faded.

She wiped a tear away with her hand, leaving a black smudge on her face. There was a beaten look about her when she said, "Despite my doubts about Richard Cooper, I shouldn't be alone. I'm going to marry him."

The words were no sooner out of her mouth when the sky turned black and ominous. Anger rose within her. She would not make it home before the storm.

She raised her head irritably and yelled into the wind, her entire body shivering.

"Why is this happening to me? Am I cursed?"

She heard Brooks bark and whine, but paid little attention. The fight had gone out of her, and her body felt cold and stiff. She fell, and hard gusts of wind blew debris and leaves on her. Suddenly, the gate clanged loudly, jolting Stephanie back to her senses.

For a moment, she thought she saw ghostly apparitions. "Grandmother?" she murmured as she followed the apparitions slowly towards the gate. Once she stepped out the gate, it slammed shut, and she found herself on the dark hillside all alone, unable to see anything at all as the wind whipped against her face.

That's when she realized Brooks was missing.

"Brooks," she called out in a loud voice as the wind whipped against her face.

She thought she heard a horse snort, but it was so dark she couldn't see anything. She told herself that her mind must be playing tricks on her.

She felt a surge of panic when she heard hooves racing toward her at full speed. The phantom rider seized her, clamping her in a vice-like grip.

"Who are you?" she gasped.

His voice was deep. "It doesn't matter who I am. Do you not know that you are in the middle of a storm without a lantern to guide you?"

They were traveling at a fast speed. It was as if the horse's hooves were not touching the ground, but flying.

"My dog," she yelled out against the wind. "I have to go back for my dog."

"Your dog is fine," he said in a gruff voice.

At that moment, Brooks barked.

"Thank God," Stephanie said.

The horse snorted.

The phantom rider dropped her at the door. She squinted her eyes at the wind and rain and could barely make out his form. His black cape whipped about in the wind. The horse was larger than any she'd ever seen before.

"Go in and light your lanterns. Stay warm. And never venture out on a night like this again. You were in grave danger. Do you understand?"

"Yes," she said, sounding like an obedient child.

"Go," he commanded.

Stephanie ran to the door and pushed against the heavy gusts until it opened, and Brooks slumped in, wet and exhausted, throwing himself down on the rag rug in front of the door. She had just slammed the door behind them when the storm hit in full force.

Stephanie went to the pantry, brought out two kerosene lamps, and lit them. And built fires in the fireplaces in case she lost power. Her phone was beeping a storm alert, and the wind was howling. She felt chilled and made sassafras tea. Then she settled back on the loveseat in front of the fireplace, covering her legs with a white knitted throw. Only then did she grasp the full realization of what had happened. And it spooked her.

"It's all about the black book, isn't it?" she said out loud to herself. She wasn't supposed to read it, but she knew it was just a matter of time until curiosity would get the best of her, and she would go on to the next chapter.

A shiver went down her spine as she thought about the phantom horseman. His voice had been deep and commanding. It had to be Damien; her prince charming. He saved her.

She sighed and threw back the throw, too excited to sleep.

In minutes, she was lumbering up the steps to her bedroom with Brooks at her heels. She lit candles, threw some wood on the fire, then sat down in the easy chair in front of the fireplace.

Stephanie gently opened the black book. All I want is a glimpse of his face before I go to sleep, she told herself. I need one look. He sounded so manly, so strong. He picked me up as if I were as light as a feather. I must admit, I am wildly attracted to him. It's wrong—he's a dark prince. A smile tugged at her lips in anticipation as she leafed through the book, skimming over chapters that she'd already read—the stroke of the quilled pen strong—the lines as black as sin. She felt elated when she found his picture.

"Thank you for saving me tonight," she said in a whisper.

His smile grew broad.

In an instant, she thought she heard breathing. It was so subtle. She felt her heart pound. Her eyes grew wide when she heard the beat of her heart synchronize with the black book. Then she grew calm.

She felt his warm lips on hers. He kissed her all over her face.

"You must rest, my darling," he murmured.

"This isn't real," she said.

"No, no. It's only a fairy tale. But you must promise never to go out in a storm again."

Stephanie drifted into a dreamless sleep, exhausted. And even though she knew it was only a picture in a book, the kiss had been real. She was grateful for the comfort the black book gave her.

She could never give it up.

Never.

The Rolltop Desk

The winter doldrums ended, and spring arrived. Stephanie was up early, eager to begin her day. She took a shower, made a peach pie, and took Brooks for a walk. She looked up on the hill at Stratford Place, awed by the beauty, the opulence—the manicured lawn, rose gardens, and wildflowers blooming in the surrounding spacious fields. Then she went to her rose garden and trimmed the roses. She thought about how she and Thomas's brother, Jacob, used to garden together. She missed him. But most of all, she missed Thomas.

Later, Richard came by for dinner, and they invited Bradley, his assistant. Richard grilled steaks. She made a salad and baked potatoes, and they had wine with dinner and an apéritif of sherry afterward.

Bradley helped her clean up, while Richard answered messages. She enjoyed having Bradley there. She knew he was loyal to Richard and an exceptional personal assistant. Still, he had also become a good friend and companion, providing good company when Richard was out of town. He was the one who asked her about her day, how she felt about the smallest, most insignificant things. And against the backdrop of the sometimes-gloomy estate, he brought a ray of sunshine. Most of all, he was her confidant.

Bradley and Thomas's assistant, Adam, knew each other. When Richard was out of hearing distance, she asked him if he had played chess with Adam. It turned out that he had, and she ventured further. "Did you see Thomas?"

she asked.

"I did. We talked. He's miserable," Bradley said, clamping up when Richard came back into the kitchen. Stephanie forced a smile, excused herself, and went to her room. She locked herself in the bathroom and cried heart-wrenching tears.

Life with Richard was good, and they were getting along better. The wedding plans were underway, and on the surface, everything seemed to go smoothly. But secretly, she was tormented and wounded from memories of her star-crossed boyfriend, Thomas Shrock.

She busied herself with endless projects around the house. When she pulled out her worn notebook, there were notes and drawings in Thomas's hand from past projects that she and Thomas had worked on together. They were her treasures. Love divided. Unfairly. Richard always seemed to come up short.

She worked diligently, with unswerving conviction and concentration on renovating the house. One day, she glanced out the window and saw a delivery truck from Fritz and Thomas, and then heard a knock at the front door. She heard Becca answer the door and called down, "What is it, Becca?"

"Thomas had a desk delivered for you. Where do you want it?"

Stephanie stood shaken at the top of the stairs. "Bring it upstairs to my bedroom," she stammered. Her hand on her pounding heart, as she watched Jacob and Sawyer heft the massive cherry rolltop desk up the stairs. They moved her small desk to the other side of the room and placed the new one against the wall near the window.

After the roll-top desk was placed perfectly, Jacob said, "Thomas made it himself. It's for you to do your writing. There's a secret drawer on the top right. He told me to tell you he left a letter in there for you."

Curious, Stephanie placed her hand against the smooth cherry wood, and the secret drawer slid open ever so slightly.

"Don't open it now," Jacob said. "Thomas said it's private."

"It's a beautiful desk," Stephanie said, marveling at the quality. "I can't thank him enough. There aren't enough words to describe how much this means to me."

"You might marry Thomas in the church," Jacob said, his expression deadpan.

Stephanie paled and bit her lip.

"We should go," Sawyer said. He turned to Jacob and said, "Wait for me in the truck."

Stephanie grabbed Jacob by the arm as he turned to leave and said, "Ask Becca to get you some cookies and milk. There's fresh milk in a crock in the refrigerator with a dipper." Unable to contain her emotions, she hugged him. "You look so much like Thomas did at your age. You've got the same gray eyes, but you're a little taller."

"Yah. Everyone says that. I'm not a little boy anymore. I'm going to my first Rumspringa Saturday."

"You're all grown up. Do you have a girlfriend?"

"Yep. Her name's Adeline. She's English like you," Jacob said. "You should come to Rumspringa with Thomas and meet her."

"An English girl? Do Fritz and Emily know that you're dating an English girl?"

"Yep. I'm not cowardly about it… like some people I know."

Stephanie turned crimson.

"Go have your cookies and milk," Sawyer said. "I'll be down in a few minutes."

Jacob needed one more word. "You've got to stand up for what you believe, Steph."

"Go," Sawyer said, with a tone that told Jacob he meant it.

Stephanie watched the tall, good-looking, gray-eyed boy walk out the door, knowing full well that he had repeated the exact words she had instilled in him when he was younger. She'd always told him to stand up for what he believed, and he was. But she wasn't. Jacob was right. She was cowardly.

Stephanie dropped her eyes and smoothed her dress, trying to compose herself, very much aware of Sawyer's eyes on her. She hadn't seen him since the night of the exorcism. He'd saved her life. It seemed like she should say something prophetic to him, but she felt tongue-tied.

"I hope you're doing well," Sawyer said. He spoke haltingly. "There are some quilts at my grandmother's cabin. I want you to have them. And I thought you might like to see Thunder."

"Thunder?" she asked. "Are you talking about my horse?"

"Yes, I board horses for Thomas, and I have your horse."

"Oh, I didn't know. I owe you money. I'll write you a check."

"It's not about money," Sawyer said. His voice got stronger. "I could saddle him up, and we could go for a ride down by the creek."

Stephanie smiled. He's saved her life the night of the exorcism, and she would always be grateful. "Don't you want to save the quilts for the woman you marry? I'm sure you'll marry one day, and your wife will want them."

"I'm not the marrying kind. It seems like they should go to someone special."

Stephanie wondered why he would give her his family heirlooms. "I'll come by tomorrow if that's okay," she said. "I'd love to see Thunder and go riding."

"Look forward to it," Sawyer said, tipping his hat.

Stephanie's heart skipped a beat. The feeling she'd had for him the night of the exorcism was still there.

Secrets in Nell Rhodes Closet

Stephanie turned into the gravel driveway, feeling guilty for lying to Richard about where she was going. It had been a half-truth. She'd told him that her horse, Thunder, was being boarded at a stable in Berlin, and she wanted to go by and see him.

Richard had looked at her with narrow eyes, as if he knew she was lying, and said, "Plan to bring Thunder home. You have an enormous barn, and I can't have you driving forty miles to see your horse whenever you get a whim. Why don't you wait until tomorrow, and I'll go with you?"

"Tomorrow, I'll be busy making peach jam. Mar-Jean brought peaches today, and I need to use them before they go bad. I'll be home by dinner if you want to come by. I put an English pot roast in the oven."

"No. I have an important meeting this evening. But let's get this settled about your horse. Are you going to tell the stables that you're bringing Thunder home?" he pressed. "We'll go get him next week."

"Well, I can't bring him home until I have help. It's too much for me, especially in the fall when I'm back in college, with schoolwork. They exercise him daily, groom him, and the stables are very reasonable."

"What do you pay?" Richard asked. "When I was going through your canceled checks, there wasn't anything written to a stable."

Stephanie's brows furrowed. "You went through my canceled checks?"

"Of course. I'm your guardian when your father is out of town. It's my responsibility, at least until you're twenty-one."

"I paid in cash," Stephanie lied, remembering that she had not paid Sawyer for boarding Thunder.

"Don't be gone all day," he said, his steel-blue eyes hinting of suspicion. "I'll worry about you."

Stephanie felt a twinge of guilt, but it would not stop her from going. She ran upstairs to a floor safe in her closet and took out a thousand dollars, and put it in an envelope. Her hands shook as she sealed it. She grabbed a sweater and ran downstairs.

Becca met her at the back door in the mudroom, holding a big bag of bruised apples. "These are for Thunder. You'd best not be gone long," she said, her lips tight. "I think Richard knows something is going on. He's meaner than usual. I heard him on the phone, yelling."

"It's just about work," Stephanie said, ignoring her warning. "Watch the roast. I have it at a low temperature. It should be fine."

Becca followed Stephanie to the car. She looked worried. "Don't go," she said. "It will cause trouble if Richard finds out where you are. And what about Thomas? You should thank him for the desk. He made it himself."

"I know, but I have to go, Becca. I'll call Thomas later. I have a million things on my mind. This is important. Sawyer has been boarding Thunder since winter, and I haven't paid him a red cent." She told herself that she hadn't lied to Becca. She had to see Thunder and pay Sawyer.

On the drive there, she thought about Sawyer. She had butterflies when she arrived and saw him walking up from the barn. He looked fresh and clean, wearing a white shirt, black suspenders, and dark trousers.

"You clean up nice," she said. He didn't have his hat on, and his dark hair had grown out, making him look boyish.

"You do, too," he said, his dark eyes scanning her. "I love the way you look in blue jeans. I see you brought apples for Thunder."

"I did, and I was going to make cookies for you, but it was a last-minute thing…and…"

"It doesn't matter," he said, cutting her off. "I'm just glad you're here."

"The place looks great. You've built a new barn. Did Thomas help you build it?"

"Yep. We had a barn raising, and I put a new bathroom in the house," Sawyer said, beaming. "My next project is a new kitchen. Fitz & Thomas will do the cupboards."

Stephanie turned and looked back at the log house. "It looks big," she said. "Have you added on?"

"Yes. I built a hobby room. I'm carving horses, and they're bringing in good money."

"How much?"

"Five thousand for each miniature horse. Marguerite set me up in a gallery in New York. I can't believe I'm making this much money doing something I love. I send them three or four miniatures a month."

Stephanie smiled. "Twenty thousand dollars a month is a lot of money. I'm proud of you, Sawyer. You amaze me."

Sawyer smiled. "I'm making hay while the sun shines."

She hugged him and linked her arm in his, excited to see his house and Thunder. Thunder swished his tail, neighed, and bumped her with his nose, happy to see her. She fed him apples.

"Want to ride?" Sawyer asked. "I can saddle him up."

"I wish I could, but I can't stay long. We should go to the cabin, and I'll look at the quilts. And I brought a thousand dollars for Thunder's keep. It could be more if you had vet bills. Did you?"

Sawyer looked puzzled. "You don't owe me anything, Steph. Thomas has paid for Thunder's keep from the very beginning. I've had a couple of vet bills for minor things, but the bills go to Thomas."

Stephanie frowned. "I did not know," she said. She wanted to ask about Thomas, but she decided against it. She could see the garden and flowers in the back of the house, and changed the subject. "The garden looks great. You've done so much. I'm so proud of you."

"Yep," he grinned. "I bought another old cabin over on Owl Creek Road that I'm fixing up. The barn is nicer than the house. I needed more pasture for my horses. I love the property."

When Sawyer shut the door, she tensed. Being alone with Sawyer wasn't a good idea. The attraction was too strong. "Well..." she said.

"I'll pop us a beer, and we'll go upstairs," Sawyer said. "The quilts are just where my grandmother, Nell, left them, stacked on the shelf. There are dresses, aprons, and hats. Take whatever you want. Granny would want you to have them."

Sawyer went to the kitchen, and Stephanie looked around the cabin. It was as neat as a pin. She gazed around, thinking that the windows could use new curtains, when a picture on the bureau caught her eye. The woman in the photo was beautiful, with long dark hair and dark eyes. She was smiling, but her eyes looked sad.

Sawyer came in and handed her a beer.

"Who is the woman in the picture, Sawyer? She's beautiful."

"My mother," he said. "She died when I was six, and my grandmother raised me."

"And your father?" Stephanie asked.

"Don't know," Sawyer replied with a hoarse voice.

Stephanie didn't want to pry. She stared at the beautiful woman in the picture, her dark eyes haunting. "What was your mother's name?"

"Susan," Sawyer said, picking up the picture and gazing into her face.

"She's beautiful," Stephanie whispered.

Sawyer held out the beer. "Want a glass?"

"Better straight out of the bottle," she answered, holding the tip of the bottle, leaning back, and letting it stream down her throat. "This is good," she said, smiling. "Nothing like a cold beer on a hot, muggy day."

"Got plenty in the icebox," he said. "And more in the springhouse. How long can you stay?"

"I'm good for an hour. I have a roast in the oven for dinner."

"That's not long, Steph. I'd hoped we'd have more time together."

They went upstairs, and she felt a sense of reverence when she went into the closet as if she were in church. Everything was neat, and the quilts were stacked on top of each other. The cotton dresses hung on wire hangers all in a row. There was a sewing box on a shelf, and a bunch of letters held together by a ribbon. There were three shoe boxes and a pair of well-worn house slippers on the floor of the closet.

Sawyer reached up and pulled down the quilts, placing them on the bed.

Stephanie's eyes were bright as she ran her hand over the top of the quilt. "They're beautiful. Look at the tiny stitches, so straight and even."

"They're yours," Sawyer said, looking pleased that she liked the quilt. "Take whatever you want."

Stephanie went to the next one and ran her hands over it. "This one looks a lot like the one my grandmother had in the mule chest. It's called The Secret Drawer quilt. My grandmother's quilt held a letter. Some hold recipes." Stephanie said, smiling, as she searched for the secret drawer, and there it was—she pulled out an envelope. "It's a letter, and it looks very old." She handed it to Sawyer.

"It looks like my grandmother's handwriting," he said. "I'm almost afraid to open it."

"Open it," Stephanie said, smiling. "It's a treasure. I would do anything to have a letter from my grandmother written in her handwriting."

Sawyer stared at the letter in disbelief. "Do you want me to read it to you?"

"It might be best." He handed her the letter, yellowed with age, and she opened it and read.

Dear Sawyer,

Your mother didn't want me to write this letter. But my time on earth is growing short, and I think you need to know who your father is. It might shock you to find that he isn't a Mennonite. And you must not feel bad about him because he never knew about you. He's married. And your mother didn't want him to know.

Your father is a wealthy man of great importance. Your mother was his housekeeper. His name is Judge Daniel Stratford, the man you hate and fear more than anyone in your life. I couldn't tell you when you were going through all the trouble with the law. He gave your mother ten thousand dollars, and she never spent a dime. That's how I paid the fines he imposed. There are nine thousand dollars taped under the floorboard in the closet. She asked me to give it to you when you were older to provide you with a good start in life. You can do what you want, son, but a boy needs to know who his father is.

Your mother told me he's a good man, and she loved him. She never felt like you were a mistake and said you were the best thing that ever happened to her. I'd never seen her so happy as she was when you were born. You've been a blessing to me. You've worked hard since you were six years old, chopping wood, mending fences, hunting in the dead of winter, bringing in enough food for both the neighbors and me. I know you will succeed in life.

I will love you always,
Granny

Stephanie hid her shock. The man who had saved her life at the exorcism had been her brother. The tears she had been holding back streamed down her face. When her eyes met Sawyer's, his hands were covering his eyes, and his face was wet. She felt an overwhelming need to comfort him.

"Come here," she said, reaching her arms out to him. Sawyer fell into her arms, and Stephanie rocked him as if he were a child, running her hands down his back to soothe him. It seemed natural when they fell back onto the bed, intertwined in each other's arms.

She felt his tears on her neck. "It's all right, Sawyer," she murmured. "I'm glad your grandmother wrote the letter. It's true, a man needs to know who his father is, even if it isn't who he wanted him to be. It will take some getting used to, but I'm okay with it."

He spoke in a choked voice. "I wish I'd never found the letter. I don't want to offend you, Stephanie, but I don't relish the idea of being Judge's son. It scares the hell out of me. And I sure don't want to be your brother. I'm an accused murderer. I don't want to bring shame to you, Steph."

"It's a good thing, Sawyer. We'll take the letter to Daddy. He's always wanted a son. And I know he'll be fair. You're a Stratford, and you deserve what is yours."

"It's not about the money, Steph. I want nothing from him. I've earned my way, and I'm proud to have brought myself up by my bootstraps. I should burn the letter. My mother didn't want Judge to know, and I feel the same. I'm a Mennonite. It would never work."

Stephanie looked pensive. "You're a good man, Sawyer, and we have to tell him."

Sawyer was at a loss for words.

It was getting late. She knew she had to go, but she didn't trust Sawyer with the letter. She was determined to show it to her father.

"I know you're in shock," Stephanie said. "We'll talk again after you give it a chance to sink in." She hugged him goodbye, but he didn't hug her back.

He sighed and put his hand over his forehead. "You should go. I want to be alone. I'm going to need some time to digest this."

She got up, grabbed the quilt, then snatched up the letter off the table and tucked it between the folds of the quilt.

"I'll call you later," she said as she dashed away down the steps and out the door.

She held back the tears until she got to the end of the drive, and then she cried a river of tears. She had to show the letter to her father, but first, she had to deal with Richard, who would be furious because she was late. Life had been easy before Richard, when all she had to fear was the wrath of her father.

Now that she was late, she would have to make up another lie.

God, how she hated lies.

Guilt Ridden

It was five o'clock when she drove in the driveway at Brighton House, a place that had been her refuge in troublesome times until Richard moved in. She was late and braced herself for the tongue-lashing she was about to receive.

Stephanie knew something was wrong when she walked into the kitchen and saw Brooks lying in the corner, his ears back, and curled up tightly, as if he was trying to make himself as small as possible. Boots was nowhere to be seen. She checked the roast, and it appeared to be fine. There weren't any plates in the sink or on the table, so she knew Richard and Bradley had not eaten. She thought they must be in the library working. She grabbed her apron and set the table.

When Richard yelled her name from upstairs, she froze, then ventured up the steps, barely able to breathe. She paused by the bedroom door and saw him throwing clothes into a suitcase.

"Where the hell were you?" he asked, the streak of cruelty that he hid in public coming out. "I called you three times."

"I took a long ride on Thunder and lost track of time," she lied. "Why are you packing? Are you leaving for New York?"

"No. Dad's in Riverside Hospital," he said in a stressed voice. "He had a heart catheterization and has three blockages. They're getting him ready for surgery. Your parents are there, my mother, and the priest. When you didn't answer your cell phone, I was worried. I should have left half an hour ago."

"The priest is there?" she asked in disbelief. Guilt flooded her entire being.

"It's serious, Stephanie. He might not make it."

"I'll get ready to go. It won't take me long."

"No. Someone has to be here with your menagerie," Richard said sarcastically. "Bradley had to fly to New York to assist on a case."

Richard's words struck her hard. She loved Parker, and Richard was punishing her — speaking to her in a disrespectful and unkind way, but she tried not to get rattled. "I'm sorry I was late. Can I get you something to eat before you go?"

"No, I can't eat at a time like this." His voice was cold and curt.

She told herself she would not yield to the pressure she was feeling. "Richard, please let me do something. Don't shut me out."

"If you want to do something for me, you can start by staying home instead of gallivanting all over the country." He threw a pair of socks into the suitcase and turned to her; his tone was sharp. "You come with a lot of baggage, Steph—a cat, a dog, a horse, and your housekeeper is a bitch."

That's when she lost it. She could feel the heat rising to her neck as she lashed out. "It might help if you would try to get along with Becca. I'm lucky I still have a housekeeper. You complain about every little thing." Then it occurred to her he might have abused Brooks. "Did you do something to Brooks? He's in the corner with his ears back."

"I yelled at him and shoved him away with my foot. He was barking—he saw a rabbit out the window and wanted to chase it. Becca was nowhere to be seen. I won't cater to your animals. You can't just take off whenever you want and leave me with all of this. Do you have any idea how much money I make and what my monthly payroll is? I have to keep the ball rolling. I can't babysit your animals."

Stephanie put her hands on her hips and strode up to him. "I don't need you to babysit my animals, and I couldn't care less how much money you make. Rich or poor, you're the same man, Richard—an egotistical ass. I want you out of my house."

Richard feigned shock. "Thanks for the sympathy, Steph. My father is about to have heart surgery, and you're arguing with me. You are such a spoiled brat. I suppose you are going to tell your father that I started it."

Stephanie glared at him, her green eyes flashing. "Of course, I'm telling my father everything. He needs to know what you do to my animals when I'm away. You're not the man he thinks you are—"

Richard leaned into her face, cutting her off. "Let me tell you something, 'Little Miss High and Mighty.' Your father is not a saint. He cheated on Marguerite with his Mennonite housekeeper. And when he couldn't stand the guilt, he adopted a baby—you!"

As soon as the words tumbled out of his mouth, his face told her he wished he could take them away. "I'm sorry, I didn't mean to…"

Stephanie crumbled. Closed her eyes tight, unable to look at him. *She wondered how many secrets the family held. He knew about Sawyer's mother, Susan. But he had to be lying about her being adopted. Surely, her grandmother would have told her.*

"That's a lie, Richard. Why in the world would you say such a thing? Isn't it enough that you want to strip me of my self-esteem? Must you strip me of my name, too?"

"I'm sorry," he said. "I was angry. I didn't mean it."

"It's too late to say you're sorry. You've already done too much. You're a monster."

"Hey! I apologized," Richard lashed out. "I would expect some respect. Do you even know the meaning of humility?"

"Do you?" Stephanie sniffed as she turned on her heel and dashed out of the room.

Dejected, Stephanie trudged downstairs and dropped on the dog bed with Brooks. She gathered him in her arms. "Never mind him, Brooks; he's a monster. I let a monster move into the house. Can you ever forgive me?"

Richard heard her as he came bounding down the steps. "A monster? I'm a monster?" he parroted. "That's another thing. I'm tiring of losing sleep at night, chasing your boogie man away."

"You've never lost a night's sleep in your life," Stephanie huffed. "You leave Bradley to take care of me because your work is more important."

"Bradley works for *me*, Steph," Richard yelled. "He's my assistant, not your dog-sitter."

"For God's sake, go," Stephanie said in a hateful voice. "And don't come back."

For a moment, she thought he looked hurt. Maybe she'd been too harsh, but she'd wanted to hurt him like he'd hurt her.

It seemed forever until she heard Richard roar away in his BMW, tires screeching. She sighed a long sigh of relief. Her anger at Richard was consuming every ounce of her energy.

She knew she could never take back the angry words she had spoken. If only her grandmother were here. Oh, how she wished they could have one of their 'talks' — if only—she could hear her sweet voice one more time. Stephanie trudged into her grandmother's bedroom and threw herself across the bed. She buried her head in the billowy pillow. Her grandmother's flowery scent still filled the room.

"I'm sorry," she said, drowning in guilt. "Bradley and Becca were both here when I left. How could I know Parker would have an emergency?" She heaved a sigh, then rambled. "I'm not good at relationships, grandmother. I find them confining. A girl should be free, shouldn't she? I had to go to Sawyer's. How could I not?"

Brooks came to the bedside and whined.

"Okay, you're hungry," she said. "I'm hungry, too."

Stephanie trudged to the kitchen with Brooks at her side, trying to understand why Richard felt burdened by her animals. It was never a big deal for her father to multitask, walking around the kitchen with the phone to his ear while letting the dog out, and making her a snack when she was little. Their pets were like family members. Her father read the paper every night with their big brown lab, Brandy, at his feet. She had mistakenly believed that Richard would be like her father. She was discovering new and unexpected sides to Richard's character. And the more she knew, the more she disliked him.

After consoling Brooks, Stephanie ate dinner and had a small glass of wine to calm her. It felt strange being at the house alone during a crisis. Nothing seemed important at that moment except family, and she had an overwhelming desire to get in the car and drive to the hospital. She was close to packing an overnight bag when Richard called.

"How is Parker?" she asked in a small voice.

"Not good," Richard said. "They just wheeled him into the operating room. We're in the waiting room, huddled together — waiting on pins and needles."

His anger had diminished, but there was still an edge to his voice. His father was gravely ill; she told herself she would try. "I wish I were there. Tell him I love him."

"They will sedate him after surgery, and he wouldn't know you were here even if you did come. I'm spending the night here. They're only allowing my mother and me in his room. Daniel and Marguerite are going to a hotel across the street. I know you hate hotels."

She put all her anger aside, her demeanor softening as she tried to separate the contradictory emotions. "I love Parker, and I would come to be with the family as your friend."

"What the hell?" he raged. "Are you breaking up with me right before my father goes to surgery? We are having a family emergency here—Stephanie. This is a crisis. How much do you think I can take?"

His tone was abrasive.

"The last thing Dad said when they wheeled him into the operating room was that he wanted to get it over with, and get well, so he could dance at our wedding, and go on the cruise. I was holding his hand when they were wheeling him into the operating room."

Stephanie's eyes welled with tears. "Oh, God. Tell him I love him. I would give anything to be there."

"I'll call you as soon as I know something." His voice was curt when he hung up the phone.

"I'm sorry, Richard," she said to dead space, putting the phone down on the table.

The enormity of it all was overwhelming, and for a moment, she wanted to escape. She closed her eyes and whispered, "I wish I were anywhere but here. Richard is ruining my life."

She could not know that before the night was over, her wish would come true.

The Note

The drawing room was cozy with its blazing, crackling fire. Stephanie put her feet up on the ottoman and sipped a cup of decaffeinated coffee. Boots lay in her lap, contented. The English pot roast had been delicious. She was feeling better, but Parker weighed on her mind, and she'd prayed for his recovery.

The phone rang, breaking the silence. Stephanie reached over and picked it up, hoping for the best, but expecting the worst.

"How are you?" Thomas asked.

Stephanie smiled, feeling a glow at the sound of his voice.

"I'm fine. It's good to hear from you, Thomas."

"I was wondering how you like the desk."

"I love it," she said. "It's beautiful. Thank you."

"Did you read the note in the secret compartment?"

"Not yet. It's been a little crazy around here. I suppose Emily told you that Parker Cooper is in Riverside Hospital, recovering from heart surgery."

"Mother told me. How's Parker doing? I thought you might be at the hospital." He paused. "You were on my mind, so I thought I would call."

"Only immediate family may see him, or I would be there," she said.

"Are you okay?" he asked. "Your voice sounds sullen."

"I'm fine. It's just that Parker has been like my second father, and I'm worried about him. Daddy and Marguerite are at the hospital. A lot has gone on—Richard and I had a falling out. We were not on good terms when he left for the hospital."

"I'm sorry if he upset you. Can I do anything?"

"I'm feeling better. How about you? Are you with anyone?"

"Kinda. I heard you and Richard set the date.

Stephanie stared into the fire, hot with jealousy.

"Well, you know, Thomas—if you're seeing someone—I don't think you should gift me with expensive furniture," she bristled. "A roll-top desk is an enormous gift."

"I made it myself," he said. "I wanted you to have something special to remember me by."

His words tugged at her heart, her anger dissipating. "How could I forget you, Thomas? I've known you all my life. I have so many wonderful memories."

"Don't talk about me like I'm dead."

"Well, if you're with someone, and I'm with Richard, it's over with us. Stop pretending that it isn't."

"This conversation is not going the way I had hoped," Thomas said in a downtrodden voice. "I thought the desk might have meaning for you since you plan to be a writer, but you're telling me I shouldn't have made it."

Stephanie wiped a tear. "Every time I look at it—I'll think of you. And I don't know if I can handle it."

"So, what do you do with those feelings, Stephanie? Do you stuff them away inside of yourself to be dealt with years later—when you find out you made the biggest mistake of your life? Are you going to go through life doing what your father wants, and not what *you* want?"

"It isn't just Daddy. It's a social stigma. You know as well as I do that an English girl and an Amish man won't work. It would drive us apart."

"Only if we let it," Thomas said. "My mother raised you as her own. You were an 'insider' from the time you were an infant. When you went to college, you changed. You left me. I didn't leave you."

The accusatory way he said it hit her like a ton of bricks. "Our lives took different directions," she quipped. "You became a deacon, and I'm working on a degree in English Literature."

"We could make it work."

"I'm not seeing it, Thomas. Your people have shunned me."

"Shunning doesn't last forever. It's temporary," he said in a gentle voice.

"The hurt is too great," Stephanie said. "I don't think I can ever forgive them."

Thomas heaved a sigh. "I'm a deacon, and I can't convince the woman I love that forgiveness will heal her pain."

Stephanie drew back. "You've never told me you loved me, Thomas."

"You knew it. And don't pretend you didn't."

His words inflamed her. "You've never kissed me, but I suppose you've kissed other girls hundreds of times, and I heard you took Maddie to the barn. You—a deacon."

"I wanted it to mean something when I kissed you. I wanted it to be special. But we never got there, Stephanie."

"But you got there with Maddie!"

"You'd do well to stop pointing fingers," Thomas said in a calm, even voice. "Everyone in Brier Hill County knows that Richard Cooper won't date a woman unless she 'puts out.'"

It was like a slap in the face.

Stephanie slammed down the phone.

And then she sobbed—long, heart-wrenching sobs that turned into a river of tears.

A half hour later, she pulled herself off the love seat in the drawing room and lumbered up the stairs to her room.

She opened the secret drawer of the roll-top desk and took out the letter written on plain, lined notebook paper with a blue ball-point pen.

Stephanie sat down, put her hand to her heart and read:

Dear Stephanie,

I hope you like the desk. It's made from the finest oak wood. Memories came back as I created the desk. It took me back to when I carved our initials on the oak tree. You were only fifteen, and I was eighteen, but I knew you were the girl for me. You're the only girl I've ever wanted.

When I see you, my heart skips a beat. And the sound of your voice makes me feel happy. It makes the entire day better.

I have a lot of regrets. I know I should have told you I loved you, but I thought you knew because of my actions. I have done everything possible to show you. I can't name everything I've made for you—there are too many, but I think you love the craft room.

If you love me, Stephanie, you will do what I ask regarding the black book. Lock it up in the antique desk where you found it. I know the book is evil.

I put my whole heart into this desk. One day, I'll pass you on the street and say, "That's Stephanie Stratford, a famous writer. I used to know her..."

I'll never forget you.

Thomas

Stephanie heaved a sigh, held the letter to her heart, and cried. Then she put her head down on the desk, running her hand across the surface, as her tears spilled over on the strong oak wood, as Brooks lay at her feet, whimpering.

Twenty minutes later, she locked the black book away in the antique desk and whispered, "I love you, Thomas."

Later that night, she saw a light on in the guest cottage and saw Bradley's car in front of the cottage. She heaved a sigh, glad he was back from his trip.

Minutes later, he called. "I talked to Richard earlier, and Parker is doing much better. He's out of surgery and in recovery. "

"I'm so relieved. I was thinking of going there tomorrow morning," Stephanie said.

"He still has visitor restrictions," Bradley said. "Only the immediate family may see him."

"I suppose Richard told you we had an altercation."

"Yes. He feels terrible about the outburst. He has a hair trigger temper—can't take pressure. Is there anything I can do?"

"No," Stephanie said. "It's been a tough day. I'm going to bed."

"Let me know if you need anything," Bradley said. "I'll be up for a while, unwinding from the trip."

"I'm fine," Stephanie said. "I'll see you tomorrow."

Stephanie had slept until nine a.m., then had a leisurely breakfast and took a shower. It was a comforting feeling, knowing Bradley was in the guest cottage.

Stephanie could hear the whir of the vacuum as Becca moved from room to room. Everything seemed to get back to normal — until she heard a sharp knock on her bedroom door.

Stephanie flung open the door, and Becca stood, looking pale.

"When I went into the library to vacuum, the secret drawer of the desk was open," Becca said. "It's always shut and locked."

Stephanie ran downstairs to the library with Brooks at her heels.

It was just as Becca had said. The secret door was wide open.

Stephanie peered inside, and the black book was gone.

"Should I call the sheriff?" Becca asked.

"Not yet," Stephanie said. "Maybe whoever has it will bring it back."

Then she called Bradley and told him about the theft. Since there hadn't been a sign of a break-in, Bradley thought that Becca may have done it to create drama.

"No, it wasn't Becca," Stephanie protested. "I know when she's lying."

"Maybe it's for the best," Bradley said. "Richard never liked the book."

Stephanie took a cup of green tea up to her room, sat down at her desk, looked out over the rolling hills, and wrote—the pen flying over the paper.

I know Thomas has the book. No one else would have taken it. He knew it was evil, yet he took it to protect me. It could have unleashed a thousand demons upon him.

After rummaging through a couple of drawers, Stephanie found her grandmother's rosary in her grandmother's bedside stand. She held the rosary, made the sign of the cross, and said a prayer for Thomas. Feeling anxious, she went to the garden and pulled weeds. Gardening always helped her with anxiety.

Stephanie stood when she heard the roar of a car engine. She shielded her eyes from the sun and saw the sheriff's car with its red light going around in a circle. He came to a screeching stop in front of the door and jumped out of the car.

Wiping a bead of sweat off her brow with the back of her hand, Stephanie walked out to meet him. She could tell by the sheriff's expression that something was wrong. Before she could speak, he said, "There's been an accident. Thomas Shrock almost died. He's asking for you."

Her hand went to her heart. "Thomas," she said, breathless. "What's happened to Thomas?"

"He tried to commit suicide. He's going to be okay, but it was a close call. Jacob went to the barn and found Thomas with a rope around his neck. He was in the saddle with his heels dug into Betsy's side. Betsy wouldn't move. Thank God, he's alive. There was some injury when Jacob was getting him down. Most of the injuries are rope burns.

Stephanie screamed. "This can't be happening." She looked up into the sky and shouted at the evil entity she now knew was in the black book. "What have you done? What have you done to Thomas?"

Bradley came running. "What's going on?" he asked the sheriff.

"Thomas Shrock tried to hang himself. He's going to be okay, but he has bad neck burns, and he's asking for Stephanie.

A look of shock crossed Bradley's face.

Becca heard the ruckus and came running.

"I have to go," Stephanie said in a choked voice. "Thomas Shrock has tried to hang himself."

"I'll drive you," Bradley said.

They followed the sheriff with his red light and siren blaring. She was embarrassed as the villagers gawked as they drove through Brier Hill. She leaned closer to Bradley, as if to shield herself from their stares. It was as if they all knew where she was going and blamed her for Thomas's attempted suicide.

"Don't look at them," Bradley said. "They don't mean any harm. They're just nosy."

Stephanie put her hand across her forehead. "Thomas is a deacon, a peace-loving man who follows the Old Amish doctrines. The Amish believe you will go to hell if you kill yourself. Something drove him to do it."

The Confession

Stephanie could see the black book in the middle of the pentagram when they pulled into the drive at Thomas's. Fear-stricken, she mustered up the courage to shout. "I'm the one you want. Leave them alone."

The Amish stood on the hill at the main house, looking down at her. It was intimidating to see the Amish all together in black, casting hateful stares at her. They blamed her. The horse and buggies parked neatly in rows reminded her of the night of the exorcism.

The sheriff and his deputy walked beside her, carrying rifles. Bradley took her arm, and they started the long walk up the hill. Her heart pounded. *Would they let her through?*

"Move back," the sheriff demanded. "Thomas wants to see Stephanie."

They parted like the Red Sea, though she heard some muttering about witches and a book.

Emily led Stephanie to the upstairs bedroom where Thomas lay, wearing an ice collar around his neck, his face ashen. She sat on the edge of the bed, holding his icy hand, her face wet with tears.

"Why?" she asked in a broken voice.

"I don't know what came over me," Thomas said, his voice parched. "I've never had such dark thoughts. It was a foolish thing to do."

Stephanie held a glass of water to his lips. He took a sip, then shut his eyes as if he were too weak to hold them open. Looking across the room at

Bradley, sitting quietly, Stephanie knew what she had to do.

"Thomas," she said softly, "Did you take the black book from the desk?"

"Yes," he said in a low voice. "I thought it was best. It was evil. I had to do it, and I'll never be sorry. It's hard to talk, but I'm going to tell you everything. Confession is good for the soul."

Stephanie stood with her arms folded as if she was trying to protect herself from what she was about to hear.

Thomas was about to confess his grave sin to her because that's what the Amish did. If they wronged, they confessed their sin. Thomas spoke in a serious voice, choosing his words carefully. "It pains me to tell you the story because it's horrible. What I saw last night was so shocking that it changed me. I'll never be the same person."

Stephanie's brows furrowed, afraid of the tale he was about to tell.

"After I called you and found you had not destroyed the black book, I took matters into my own hands. I went to your house at three a.m. and stole the book. I had a key that Hedy had given me years ago. Brooks heard me, but he didn't bark because he knew me. I gave him a bone."

Stephanie sat rigid, her heart beating loudly. She could hardly believe that Thomas dared to do such a thing.

"I was on my way to burn that book in the trash bin by the barn when something…unnatural happened," Thomas said. "The book just…lifted itself and landed right in the middle of that pentagram. Then a gust of wind came from nowhere, and when the book fell open…a man stepped out of it."

Stephanie felt her breath catch. So she'd been right all along—the book truly was magical, and capable of bringing its illustrations to life.

"This wasn't just any man," Thomas continued, his voice dropping. "He looked like nobility from centuries past—fine stockings, breeches, a velvet coat fit for a king. I stood there, and he looked right at me and thundered my name: 'Thomas Shrock.'"

"I couldn't move, couldn't speak. My feet wouldn't obey when I tried to flee. He said I had no chance against him, that you were already his. Called me a thief who'd committed a terrible sin. When I offered to return the book, he refused, saying only that you should handle it. Then he vanished—just smoke where he'd stood. I left everything untouched and warned everyone away."

"The bishop believes we shouldn't destroy the book, so I reached out to Mazie Moon. It's as if the devil himself is loose in Brier Hill County."

Stephanie's throat tightened as the question burned inside of her. *Had her cruel words driven Thomas to such desperation?*

"The hanging," she whispered. "Was it because of what I said about your book?"

Thomas shook his head. "The book itself—it planted something dark inside me. Like being possessed. I couldn't fight it."

A voice floated through the window, each syllable of her name stretched thin and hollow. "Steph-a-nie... Steph-a-nie..."

The blood drained from Thomas's face. His fingers clamped around her wrist. "That's Damien. Don't answer him. Stay here where it's safe. We'll pray—prayer has power against his kind."

"He's after me, Thomas. If I hide, who pays the price next? Look what he made you do." She glanced toward the window. "There are hundreds of people out there. Children. I can't risk their lives."

"Please," Thomas begged, clutching her hand.

Stephanie tore free and bolted for the door.

Bradley planted himself in front of her, the veins in his neck bulging. "You're not going out there. I just saw them through the window—a sorceress with seven witches forming a pentagram. Whatever dark magic they've summoned, let them handle it themselves."

Emily appeared in the doorway, her face pale. "It's not their doing, Bradley. When the Judge adopted Stephanie, only he and Hedy knew about the curse. A wizard bound her to a dark prince at birth. The monks' protective seals are breaking. If the prince claims her, he'll take her to his kingdom and marry her." She wrung her hands. "Hedy swore secrecy. That book—it contains power beyond understanding. Hedy only told me it needed to remain locked in the desk's hidden compartment."

Emily seized Stephanie's trembling arm. "If you step outside, the dark prince will take you. You remember Hedy's bedtime stories, don't you?"

Stephanie's nod was barely perceptible, her eyes wide with terror.

"Those weren't just stories," Emily whispered, her voice breaking as she offered a patchwork quilt. "I've done everything I could—buried the charms from your closet, sewn this Rattlesnake Quilt, prayed over every stitch for a month. Evil can't touch you beneath it." She turned to Bradley. "Tell the sheriff to bring his car to the front. She'll need to run with the Rattlesnake Quilt wrapped around her."

"No. My father didn't raise a coward," Stephanie said. "I have to go. It's me he wants."

Stephanie ran to Thomas and put her cheek, wet with tears, next to his. "You're my rock, Thomas. You've always been my rock. If I don't come back—know that I love you, and only you." And then her lips brushed his—sweet and gentle.

Stephanie knew what Thomas didn't know—they were Star-Crossed lovers. They could never be together, but she would always love him.

"Don't go," he said in a cracked voice. "We'll fight this together."

Bradly grabbed her and tried to stop her, but she broke through his hold.

"My father didn't raise a coward," she yelled, as she tore down the steps, out the door, and into the mob.

All hell had broken loose.

The Sorceress and The Seven Witches

Mazie Moon, a sorceress, had never doubted her power or that she could protect herself—until today, when she came face to face with evil at Thomas Shrock's farm in Brier Hill County. She spied the black book in the middle of a pentagram and sensed the energy coming from it when she approached. It was a pentagram that she'd drawn weeks ago.

There was an eerie feeling in the air. The Sorceress and the Seven Witches entered the pentagram and surrounded the black book. Torches blazed above their heads as they danced and chanted around the black book as if they were in a trance. They had tucked sprigs of mistletoe behind their ears, and they wore necklaces made from wood from a sacred tree. They believed plants, nature, and ancient chants would protect them.

The chanting stopped, and the sorceress stood in front of the black book. "I command you to come out of the black book, demon. I have power over you. Come out, or I will set the book on fire and destroy you."

A violent gust of wind came out of nowhere, and the sky turned from dusk to black. The black book's pages turned like a blur. The Sorceress crept close to the black book and held the torch near the pages, waiting for them to ignite.

"Burn, demon," Mazie Moon said in a mocking tone. But the pages didn't burn. She jabbed the book over and over. But the book was invincible and did not burn.

In a burst of dazzling light, Damien appeared out of the black book. He was larger than life. "You have power over nothing," Damien snarled. "A Sorceress and Seven Witches meddling with the Prince of Darkness is not a threat. You amuse me."

Mazie Moon trembled, but she did not back down. Dressed in a long black robe, she jutted her chin and stepped forward with a flaming torch. "I am Mazie Moon, a direct descendant of a Druid. My ancestors were Celtic, and my father is a priest. My magic is powerful. It is not my wish to hurt you. I only ask that you leave and take the book with you."

Damien shrugged. "I detest druids." His dark eyes were hypnotic as he approached her.

"Stay back," she warned, her eyes scanning his burgundy velvet coat, his white ruffled shirt, and breeches with long stockings. There was no question he was royalty. Though he dressed like royalty, his mouth was pure filth. He was dangerous. She drew back her torch and hurled it at him.

Damien's wicked laugh echoed throughout the hills and valleys as he grabbed the flaming torch in mid-air and waved it at Mazie. When she lifted her chin in defiance, Damien gripped her shoulder and ripped her dress with a hard yank, leaving her naked and exposed. Her face turned crimson. The Seven Witches surrounded Mazie to offer protection and began to chant and dance around her.

Damien's dark eyes glittered. He reached out and grabbed Amy by her waist-long pale blonde hair, holding the torch in one hand and her in the other.

Amy's blue eyes registered terror.

"Release her," Mazie Moon commanded.

"She's a witch. At Ludwig Castle, we burn them at the stake," Damien barked, as he threw Amy to the ground.

Amy screamed and lay whimpering, her complexion pale, and her body trembling.

Damien waved the torch, sparks flying, his long dark hair was blowing in the wind. He pointed to the black book, the pages still turning, and commanded, "Flog the witches." The book loosened from her hands and took on a life of its own.

The black book rose into the air and flew at Mazie Moon, slamming her to the ground. It pounded her over and over with brute force. She tried to cover her head with her hands and begged for mercy, but the book was relentless and beat her senseless. The Seven Witches stationed at points of the pentagram looked on in horror, powerless to save her.

When the witches turned to run, Damien used his magic and froze them on the spot. The black book beat the Seven Witches, striking them with hard blows until they were too weak to stand. They had fallen one by one. They lay groaning, afraid to move for fear it would agitate him.

Then the black book fell at Damien's feet with a thud.

"I came in peace," Damien yelled. "You're a murderous bunch of thieving heathens. A deacon stole the black book from a desk." He pointed his finger at Mazie. "You tried to burn the book. My beloved's soul is in the book, and if you dare try to destroy the black book, I will destroy you."

"I'm sorry," Mazie said in a choked voice, her black hair spilling across the pentagram, and her black dress torn. He was dangerous. She now knew that what had come from the black book was more than a demon. He was the devil himself.

Damien stood holding a flaming torch, towering over the eight women lying at his feet, battered and bloody. A smoky grey haze like burnt fog drifted above them.

Mazie Moon gazed up at Damien, her dark eyes mere slits, as she breathed in the smoke. It settled in her chest, but she dared not cough or make the slightest sound lest Damien's wrath come down upon her. Damien's anguished face called out Stephanie's name over and over, the haunting sound echoing throughout the valleys and hills.

Mazie watched as Damien's face changed from tormented to triumphant. His eyes, dark and piercing, stared at the crowd. Though she could not see Stephanie approaching, she could hear the humming of the crowd. Mazie seized the opportunity to escape and began crawling away through the damp green glass like a caterpillar. The seven witches slithered after her. They sought cover in the barn, cowering in fear, peeping out through the barn door.

"She's courageous," Mazie said as Stephanie's voice rang out into the night, shouting to the mob to 'get out of her way.' "The crowd is parting; they are heeding her commands."

"Is she a witch?" Amy asked, her voice quivering, as she watched through the crack, Stephanie walking with her head high, straight towards the evilest man alive.

"I don't know," Mazie answered, "but I sense she has powers much greater than ours."

There was complete silence as Stephanie tore down the hill and went straight to the pentagram and stood before Damien.

"I'm here," she shouted, her voice strong. "I'm the one you want. Leave them alone."

"She's sacrificing herself," Mazie said in a hushed voice, "to the devil."

Damien grabbed Stephanie's arm and pulled her into the book.

It slammed shut. The book began to rise and spin, then there was a blinding flash of light. The book vanished—swallowed up by the darkness of the night.

The Wizard and Damien

Damien stood in front of a blazing fire in his library, his eyes fiery as he shouted obscenities. "My beloved lives among heathens. A thief who professes to be a deacon stole the black book in the middle of the night. A sorceress and seven witches tried to burn the book with torches. I saved the black book with magic, and I saved Stephanie from the mob. They stoned her. Her arm was bleeding."

Wizard flew up in the air, his blue eyes flashing in anger. "If they have harmed her, I shall bring my wrath upon them."

"She's fine. Dr. Spade cleaned and wrapped the wound and gave her laudanum, and she's resting in the high tower," Damien said.

"Where is the black book?" Wizard asked. His voice held grave concern.

"Under lock and key in your den. A sorceress and seven witches tried to burn the book. And a mob stoned Stephanie. She fears the people who stoned her."

"Had they burned the book, they would reduce Stephanie to ash. The book is the heartbeat of her soul," Wizard said. "Still, you should not have been there without your army." The wizard waved his wand, agitated. "I forbid you to show your magic powers to earthlings."

"They forced me to use my magic to save the book, and I allowed Stephanie to feel the power of magic to escape the heathens."

"You are a fool to show her she has magical powers," the Wizard exclaimed.

"She can use her powers against you."

Damien looked pained. "Her heart is pure. She would not use her powers to cause harm."

"You don't know that to be true," Wizard chastised. "She's not a little girl anymore. She's a woman. I believe she has cast a spell on you."

"It's true. She's bewitched me, and I suffer from unrequited love. It's something I've never felt before. You do not know what it's like."

Wizard jutted his chin as he pointed his wand at him. "You feel vexed, discombobulated, befuddled, and wounded—as if a thousand arrows have pierced your heart. You feel unanchored and adrift in a sea of anguish and sorrow. All you can think about is her." His resounding voice echoed throughout the cavernous castle.

"It's true. I have never felt such pain."

Wizard poked Damien hard with his wand. "Don't be a fool. It doesn't befit a prince to show such weakness."

Damien snatched the wand and threw it across the room, but it shot like an arrow back at Wizard.

"The earthlings have deceived, betrayed, and almost murdered her today. We cannot put off the wedding much longer."

"Until the seal is broken, the girl will not love you."

"I put my faith in the Golden Chalice and the potion. It will cause her to lose her memory of everything—even Earth."

"There is talk among the Council that King Midas has objections. He does not believe a dark prince should wed the girl born with the golden ribbon. The rumors are that he wants her for his son, Magnus, and he will pay any price for her. It might be wise to take the gold. If he places a stumbling block in your path, it could prove catastrophic."

Damien's face grew red with anger. "I cannot sell my beloved. She is priceless. No amount of gold could give me the joy I feel when I gaze upon her beautiful face."

Wizard tapped the end of his wand on the floor. "The Feathered Pen writes. It's all in the book in my den. A mortal has kissed the girl. Why do you want her?"

Damien's expression was pensive. "Her heart is sealed. She cannot love, and her beauty and charm blind me. She's never known love. It's as though she is as innocent as a newborn lamb."

"An innocent lamb who brings men to their knees," Wizard said, his voice sharp. "Perhaps unknowingly and unwittingly—but still she does."

"That makes me feel better," Damien said through clenched teeth.

Wizard's blue eyes grew thoughtful, and he levitated until he was eye level with Damien. "I have not made the final silver charm. It is of the blessed chalice. I must make the charm before you can marry her. Dragon Helzer must fire it, and we have not seen him for several days."

Damien's face grew dark. "Well, find him! Make the blasted charm and bring it to me. We must avoid war with King Midas. Send a messenger. Tell King Midas the girl is no longer perfect."

"Tell him yourself," Wizard said. "King Midas has requested a ball—a Masquerade. While you have been away, we have been preparing a feast for the masquerade. King Midas insists upon seeing her."

"But why?" Damien raged. "It's dangerous for her to leave The Tower. The wenches could poison her. Anything could happen."

"Rumors of the *girl born with the golden ribbon* have reached all seven kingdoms. She is like a jewel. All the kings want to see her. Midas insists on seeing her golden thread that leads to the heavens."

"Only the most holy, or those with magical powers, can see the golden thread," Damien said. "Even I cannot see it."

"That's because you are dark," Wizard said, striking Damien hard across the back with his wand. "You are the darkest prince in all the kingdoms." Wizard laughed wickedly. "If your brother does not win her heart at the Masquerade, you will be fortunate."

Damien's brows furrowed. "What are you talking about?"

"King Midas has asked for games—more than a Jester, a freak, and a fortune-teller."

"What more could he want?"

"The Kissing Game. He has requested that the Queen of Hearts be present. Stephanie will kiss both you and Lucifer, and her heart will decide who will

The Wizard and Damien

have the first dance."

"King Midas has never liked me. It's an insult."

"I cannot refuse him. He brings gifts of gold." The wizard waved his wand, scattering moonbeams around the room. "One kiss. What can it matter?"

The Masquerade

A trumpet blew as Stephanie stood in the ballroom, dressed in a satin, emerald-green gown, diamonds adorning her: a magnificent diamond ring on her finger, a sparkling necklace, and matching earrings. Her pale blonde hair hung to her waist.

The trumpeter announced in a booming voice: "Stephanie Stratford from the planet Earth."

Stephanie bowed, then walked tall down the wide red carpet, with guards in full armor at her side, their swords drawn. Snitch, dressed in his finery, wore a black top hat and black vest, carrying the hem of her dress.

She'd never seen such extravagance and opulence—the ballroom filled with what looked like royalty—ladies in magnificent silk ball gowns; the flashing of diamonds. Glittering diamond chandeliers adorned the ballroom.

There were gasps among the crowd and whispers: *she is much younger than I had thought, and so beautiful.*

Wizard Anzor, the most powerful wizard in all the universe, stood in one of the tiered balconies over the platform. He sparkled: his blue eyes twinkled, and his white gown and cone hat looked as white as snow. He held his golden wand. Above the Wizard's balcony, King Midas stood all dressed in gold with his son, Magnus, at his side. They were from the wealthiest star, The Jewel Box.

You could have heard a pin drop. All eyes were on Stephanie.

Below the Wizard's balcony, on a platform... two tall, broad-shouldered, muscular men stood, all dressed in black, their faces covered in black masks. They looked ominous.

Stephanie trembled as she walked up the red carpet toward them, her head held low, unable to look at them. They looked frightening. As she neared and stepped onto the platform, each man offered her an arm. She slipped her arm in theirs. Standing between them, she felt like a lamb being led to slaughter.

She did not know which man was Lucifer, and at this moment, she hated him as much as she hated Damien. Feeling alone and betrayed, yet she did not falter. She could not chance ending up in a torture chamber or being put in the fields to work as a peasant girl. Or death itself.

She strolled as the two men led her down the wide red carpet, gazing into the crowd, her eyes darting about, hoping to find a friendly face. It was the women with black masks covering only their eyes, with thick red lips, wearing dresses that revealed their bosoms, that stood out. She believed they must be harlots from the brothel in the village—ladies of the night who had slipped in with the crowds, hoping to pick up a few coins for their favors. Their presence reminded her she could fall prey to this life if she made one wrong move.

The crowd was getting restless, and their voices rose as they talked among themselves. Wizard's voice roared above the guests. He waved his wand, his blue eyes blazing with excitement. "Let the games begin."

The room fell silent as the three stopped before an altar where a woman dressed as a card—the Queen of Hearts, dressed in a black gown with red hearts — stood, holding a blindfold. The Queen of Hearts blindfolded her and then turned her around in a circle.

Stephanie felt dizzy and was not prepared when she felt powerful arms encircle her and warm lips kiss her. Then again. But this time, sparks flew, and her heart thundered. She held on to his silk sleeve, not wanting to let go. The Queen of Hearts ripped off the blindfold, and she stood staring into the masked man's face, her mouth trembling, both in fear and excitement.

"Which kiss has won your heart, my lady?" The Queen of Hearts asked.

"The second," Stephanie said, certain it was Damien.

"What is your name?" The Queen of Hearts asked the man.

"I am Lucifer," he said in a booming voice. "The King of Darkness."

There was a hush, and then the guests talked among themselves as Lucifer led Stephanie to the dance floor.

"I knew you would choose me," he said as a smile curved his lips. His hand encircled her waist. They waltzed, the only two on the dance floor as the orchestra played, as if there were no tomorrow. He twirled her around and around in a circle, and she felt lightheaded and dizzy, as if she were under a spell.

A trumpeter sounded, sending a loud blast through the ballroom that silenced the room. And then a loud voice boomed. "Bids begin at 1000 pounds of gold."

The party continued, and a fabulous feast was served. Dancing ensued, liquor flowed, and the music played on and on.

The women were in good spirits, and the blunt manner in which they spoke took her aback. They asked her if she was in love with Damien. Before she could even answer, they would say such things as: He's a handsome devil, but he's a rake. He's broken many hearts in all the kingdoms.

Stephanie whirled from partner to partner, her feet barely touching the ground between dances, pausing only when a servant pressed a goblet into her hand. Though she sought Damien's eyes across the room, other men intercepted her, their questions oddly specific. "Do you possess a golden ribbon that reaches to heaven?" one whispered against her ear. "Tell me," another murmured, his grip too tight on her waist, "are you truly unblemished?"

Nettles hovered near the feast table, insisting that a servant taste each morsel before allowing it near her lips. "Precautions," he whispered, "for your safety."

Damien's wenches' eyes followed her with undisguised hostility.

As midnight approached, masks began slipping. Stephanie glimpsed wolfish faces, tufts of fur at their collars, eyes reflecting the torchlight like those of animals in darkness.

The Masquerade

Damien appeared at her side, his voice low. "The hour approaches. The transformation begins—man to beast. There will be howling. Blood. A sacrifice."

"Sacrifice?" The word caught in her throat.

"Shall we depart before the spectacle grows worse?" Damien extended his arm with practiced grace.

"Please," she murmured, slipping her gloved hand into the crook of his elbow. "I find it all rather barbaric."

The music swelled feverishly as dancers whirled with increasing abandon. A nobleman, his face flushed crimson, attempted to cram an entire hen down his throat while onlookers cheered.

With a subtle nod to his sentries, Damien guided her away, a dozen armed guards falling into formation behind them.

"Where are we going?" she asked, her voice barely audible above the noisy crowd.

"The Crimson Room," he said. "A chamber unknown to your innocence."

She trembled as they traversed shadowed corridors where whispers and moans echoed against stone. Flickering torchlight revealed courtesans pressed against walls, their painted lips parted in feigned ecstasy, palms gleaming with payment while gentlemen of the court rutted against them with animal urgency.

A man with bloodshot eyes swayed on his feet, rattling a dented can. "Spare a coin for a hungry soul?" As they passed, a guard's blade flashed, sending the can clattering across cobblestones. Copper pieces scattered like startled mice.

Stephanie's steps faltered, her face tightening at the harsh sound. "How could he—" She reached toward the beggar.

Damien's fingers closed around her wrist. "Leave it. I'll handle this matter later."

"But his money—" She twisted against his grip.

"Step back," Damien hissed, his eyes never leaving the beggar. "Those hands that beg will snatch that necklace from your throat in an instant."

The Crimson Bedchamber

The bedchamber was a seduction of crimson. Red velvet draperies hung from frost-painted windows, while a lone candle cast dancing shadows across the room. The massive four-poster dominated the space, its crimson spread pulled back to reveal white silk sheets that gleamed in the dim light, pillows arranged in silent invitation.

When the guards ushered them in and locked the door with an ominous click, Stephanie felt her breath catch. The danger she'd sensed at the ball was nothing compared to what lurked here, in this cavernous room, with him.

"What do you want from me?" she demanded.

Damien's smile was predatory. "Your company, of course."

"I'm not like those women in the corridor," she said, chin raised. "We aren't married. You have no claim on me."

His arms snaked around her waist from behind. "Being my mistress would elevate you. You stand alone in the world—unprotected. Men circle you like wolves, offering fortunes for a single night."

"Is that why you brought me here? To put me on display and sell me to the highest bidder?"

"The bids are substantial. Only a fool would dismiss them."

"You cannot sell me like property," she hissed. "Have you no decency?"

His fingers dug into her flesh. "Watch your tongue, or you'll feel the lash."

She flinched away, but he pressed his lips to her neck. "Such coldness from you, when I've just condemned my favorite, Bella Franz, to the dungeon on your behalf."

Stephanie whirled to face him, her forehead creased. "What are you talking about?"

"My informant discovered Bella visited the witch in the hollow tree to purchase poison. Tonight, Needles caught her bribing a servant to taint your wine—the final cup you would have drunk before retiring. If not for Lucifer's grace, you'd be dead by dawn, and she'd still warm my bed."

"Why would she want me dead?" Stephanie's voice barely carried above a whisper.

"The usual—envy, malice. Bella may be lovely, but she's venomous." His voice dropped. "They whisper 'Wicked' when she passes. The dungeon tonight, the gallows tomorrow."

Stephanie recalled the women at the party—hardly threatening in their tattered finery. They'd lingered at the edges, unmistakable despite their masks with their painted red mouths and chalk-white faces, their frayed gowns revealing bosoms. She'd glimpsed them in darkened corridors with respected men from the party.

"Your messages are unclear. In the book, you were smitten with me. You even kissed me once—the most tender kiss I've known. Yet here, face to face, you act as if I repulse you."

"Your arrogance repulses me," she said, stalling. "You have made little effort to charm me. Perhaps you should try."

"I am royalty," he boasted. "Such efforts are beneath me. Wooing or not, the night ends the same way—with you in my bed."

The hunger in his gaze made his intentions unmistakable. "I need time. We're strangers," she said, keeping her voice steady. "The ball continues. Let's return and dance—surely their ghastly spectacle has concluded."

"Dance with you?" he scoffed. "When we both know whose arms you truly seek? You chose my brother before everyone. Deception doesn't suit you." His mouth grazed the pale curve of her neck. "Your lips may deny me, but your pulse betrays you. I feel it racing against me."

That racing came from terror, not desire—from visions of what awaited her. He'd already condemned his former favorite to the dungeon's depths and spoke of selling her away. One misstep, and she'd share Bella Franz's fate: dangling from a hangman's rope by morning.

His shadow fell across her as he leaned in, extinguishing the torchlight. The wall filled with dancing silhouettes while his lips claimed hers, hot and insistent.

Tremors coursed through her body.

His fingers circled her wrists like manacles as his mouth descended to the tender hollow of her throat. His teeth grazed her skin, drawing a cry from her lips. "Are you a beast?" she gasped.

"Have you not realized?" Malice dripped from his words. "No prince awaits you here. With a word, I could see you swinging from the hangman's rope—or perhaps feel the executioner's steel where Bella's head should fall." With a savage motion, he tore the fabric at her shoulder, baring her flesh to the cold air.

She threw her hands over her breasts, horror flooding her veins. The torchlight caught the hunger in his gaze as it raked over her nakedness.

Voices rose outside, fists hammering against the wooden door.

"Cover yourself," Damien ordered, straightening his attire before cracking open the door.

The door crashed open as Lucifer stormed in, eyes sweeping the room.

"You know the code we live by," he snarled, shouldering Damien aside. "The Feathered Pen writes, and has recorded it all. The Wizard knows what you have done. And now Midas demands the girl in the ballroom."

Damien's lips curled into a cold smile. "My heart is black, and I'm a master of deceit, but I haven't touched her. If she is blemished, it was not I."

"Look at her!" Lucifer's voice thundered. "The torn gown, that mark on her neck—your signature is all over her."

"Just a love bite." Damien shrugged. "None of it matters now. I've reconsidered. She's no longer for sale."

"Midas won't accept that," Lucifer warned. "He'll bring his armies. The highest offer stands—she belongs to him now."

Stephanie remained motionless, arms crossed over her exposed chest, eyes wide with horror.

In a flurry of movement, Lillian appeared with a dark cloak, draping it over Stephanie's shoulders and covering her head before hurrying her from the room.

"What is happening?" Stephanie asked.

"King Midas is enraged that Damien took you to the Crimson Room," Lillian said as she led Stephanie down the dark halls at a fast pace. "You were to be unblemished, and King Midas has offered a ton of gold for you. He wants you for his son, Magnus, but I saw the bite on your neck. You were to be perfect."

"It's just as well," Stephanie declared. "I can't go with King Midas to the Blue Star. All of my allies are here. I would never get back to Earth."

"King Midas is a noble man, and you would have fared better with Magnus on the Blue Star than with Damien. Damien is dark, dangerous, and deceitful. He would *never* sell you. It was a ruse."

"I don't understand," Stephanie said as Lillian clutched her arm, running through the dark passageways.

"Damien believes King Midas will withdraw his bid when he sees the bite. Lucifer found out from a guard that Damien has ordered two executions tomorrow. You and Bella are to be hanged side by side."

Stephanie grew cold, but she dared not stop running. "There's a brief time when you are unguarded—Lucifer dismissed the guards. We don't have long before Damien will realize that he has left us on our own."

They ran up a winding staircase. Lillian pulled her into a dimly lit room and unlaced her dress. The beautiful, torn blue satin dress dropped to the floor, and Lillian slipped a light chemise gown over her head. Then she threw the cape over her shoulders, pulled the hood up over Stephanie's head, and tied it tight.

"He claims to love me, yet he would hang me?" Stephanie's voice trembled.

Lillian's eyes darkened. "Damien's black heart will not allow him to love you. He destroys what he touches—every woman who crosses his path. If he can't possess you, no man will." She leaned closer. "That's the true reason for the gallows."

"I believed his lies," Stephanie whispered, her world crumbling.

"We've prepared for this moment," Lillian said, fingers tracing the outline hidden in Stephanie's cloak. "I sewed the black book inside—guard it with your life. It contains your very essence. Lucifer risked everything to steal both it and the Feathered Pen from the Wizard's Den. Without them, neither Damien nor the Wizard can trace your escape or your accomplices." A smile flickered across Lillian's face. "Your chains are broken... nearly."

"But how—" Stephanie began, her thoughts scattered like leaves in a storm. "Come with me."

"We must remain behind. Damien would slaughter us all if we accompanied you." Lillian gripped Stephanie's shoulders. "At midnight, you must leap from the balcony. When The Flying Lion passes beneath you, you must jump and land on his back. Through his portal lies the path to your true love." She hesitated. "Should you fall, pray Owl catches you with his talons. Otherwise, the moat awaits—and Helser the Dragon hungers."

Stephanie's breath caught in her throat, terror freezing her blood.

"Faith is your only weapon now," Lillian whispered. "Choose—the leap or the noose that awaits Bella."

"How long do I have?" Her voice quavered.

Lillian flung the balcony doors wide. "Three minutes."

Stephanie's pulse raced as she stepped onto the balcony and scanned the diamond-studded darkness for the lion. Though invisible, his distant roar reached her ears.

"He's coming," Lillian whispered. "You'll need perfect timing to mount him mid-flight."

A sudden whoosh startled Stephanie as Owl's amber eyes materialized above.

"Now!" Owl commanded.

Without hesitation, she launched herself into the void—and landed astride the lion, fingers entwined in his thick mane as they cut through the night. His powerful muscles rippled beneath her, filling her with strength. Freedom surged through her veins—a heady, unprecedented magic.

Owl glided alongside, a guardian presence. Stephanie nestled her face into the lion's mane and heaved a sigh.

When the lion touched down on Brighton House's lawn, Stephanie tumbled onto the cool grass. Dizzy but elated, she stretched out her arms and claimed her territory once more. The fresh air filled her lungs. Home at last. Yet she wondered about Lillian's promise—the lion brought her to her true love.

Moonlight silvered the landscape, revealing a figure approaching—tall, broad-shouldered, in a crisp white shirt and dark trousers.

"Richard?" she breathed. "Is that you?"

Home, At Last

Richard swept her into his arms. "My God, I've been out of my mind with worry. Up all night, pacing. Are you hurt? And was that actually a lion on our front lawn?"

She'd forgotten how his shoulders felt—broad and solid beneath her fingertips.

"I'm fine," Stephanie said. "And yes—a lion with wings, if you can believe it."

His fingers pushed back her hood, his brow furrowing at the sight of the thin garment underneath. "These clothes..."

"A story for later," she said. "Parker?"

"Surgery went well. Discharge tomorrow."

Relief flooded through her. Then the memory of their fight resurfaced. "We need to address what happened between us, Richard. We can't pretend it away."

"I was wrong. The stress—it got to me. Never again, I swear it."

"We have much to discuss," Stephanie said. "But I need a hot bath and tea first."

"I don't want to let you go."

"You won't have to," Stephanie said. "I believe I've finally found my way back."

They have invited us

Stephanie swirled her fingers through the steaming bathwater, grateful for the simple luxury after what she'd endured. The lavender bath salts dissolved as she sank into the tub, only to be interrupted when Richard appeared with tea.

"Thank you," she said, forcing brightness into her smile.

Richard's gaze fixed on her neck, his eyes widening. His fingers brushed the wound. "This looks like an animal bite. Are you in pain?"

"He exists between worlds—man and beast both. It only stings when touched."

"We need to clean this properly," Richard said. "And start you on a course of antibiotics."

"Medicine cabinet," Stephanie murmured, suddenly exhausted. The bite seemed trivial compared to making it home alive.

Richard dabbed antiseptic on her neck. "I saw that lion. And now this bite. I have no choice but to believe your story."

The antiseptic burned, but Stephanie's thoughts had already drifted to Lillian's black book, hidden within the cloak's lining. Once Richard left to fetch toast and tea for her medication, she finished bathing and dried with a thick white towel.

The discarded cloak lay crumpled on the bathroom floor. Her fingers traced the book's outline beneath the fabric, examining Lillian's tight stitching. Unwilling to damage the garment, Stephanie locked the entire cloak in her closet safe. As long as the book remained unopened, she could pretend everything was normal.

Nestled in Richard's arms that night, Stephanie revealed everything about the barn incident with Thomas, including her declaration of love.

"Thomas will expect to marry me once he learns I've returned," she whispered.

Richard stroked her hair. "A schoolgirl crush, nothing more. You said yourself he never even kissed you. It isn't love."

"He risked his life to protect me," Stephanie said. "I owe him something."

Richard's voice was icy. "You owe him nothing. Your father said that Thomas is marrying Maddie Yoder—she's pregnant. The ceremony's in two weeks. They have invited us."

The news hit Stephanie like a bucket of ice water. Thomas and Maddie. Pregnant. The betrayal cut deeper than the marks Damien had left on her neck. Thomas had kept this secret while she poured out her heart. Perhaps his suicide attempt stemmed not from supernatural forces but from shame before her and his church, especially given his position as deacon.

Richard kissed her forehead. "Daniel suggests we attend as a family. It would silence the gossip, show our unity."

Stephanie knew immediately she would never attend. She wanted Thomas erased from her life completely. When Richard's phone rang, she flinched. It was Marsha—Parker was running a fever.

"I should go, sweetheart. My father is very ill, and my mother shouldn't be alone with him. Will you be alright by yourself?"

"Of course," Stephanie lied. "Just call me later."

His lips brushed her cheek before he vanished through the doorway.

Stephanie collapsed onto the bed, her body aching from more than just the physical wounds. The pillow muffled her sobs, but couldn't absorb the shock of Maddie's pregnancy. Thomas's wedding invitation might as well have been a death sentence.

"Why?" she whispered to the empty room. The memory of his declarations twisted into mockery. Her Star-Crossed Lover—what a cruel joke that title had become. She'd sacrificed herself for his people while he planned a future with another woman.

Each heartbeat felt like glass shards in her chest. Richard waited in the wings. The prophecy of the lion had led her to him. Perhaps fate knew better than her rebellious heart.

Sleep finally claimed her, bringing visions of diverging paths—one golden and regal, the other wild and treacherous. Thundering hoofbeats grew louder. *What was happening? Was she going to the gallows, after all?*

Bella Franz

Stephanie awoke screaming, rudely awakened by a nightmare. She saw a woman's body hanging, her head in a noose—her lifeless body swung back and forth like a rag doll. She knew instinctively it was Bella Franz. God Almighty! Damien had murdered his wench.

Stephanie ran to the bathroom and vomited. *How had it happened? How had Damien been able to reach her through a dream? Wasn't she free of him?* Mentally juggling all the events that had occurred and trying to make some sense of it, she lay on the floor of the bathroom and shut her eyes, trying to block out the image of Bella Franz hanging lifeless.

She splashed cold water on her face, then washed her face, and dried with a white towel, grateful for the fresh smell and all the comforts of home that she used to take for granted. She started when she saw her reflection in the mirror: she was pale and had circles under her eyes. And her usually shiny, well-kept blonde hair had lost its luster. She was headed for the shower with shampoo and conditioner when she heard a noise downstairs. *It has to be Becca,* but it was early for her.

Stephanie opened the bedroom door and called out, "Who's there?"

"It's just me," Daniel answered. "Parker's fever is down, and he's coming home. I was out for my morning walk and thought I'd check on you. You're up early."

"Couldn't sleep," Stephanie called back.

"I couldn't either. Saw something strange in the sky. Almost looked like a lion."

"Oh… that is strange," she stammered as she hurriedly put on her white, thick chenille robe and ran down the steps with Brooks at her heels.

Daniel had just put the teapot on the stove. "What happened to you?" he asked, eyeing her suspiciously. "You're pale, and your hair looks like you were in a windstorm."

"I must have got caught in the rain when I walked Brooks last night." She glanced at him, deceit written all over her face. "I should let Brooks out," she said, leaving the room.

"It didn't rain," Judge called after her. "You don't have to lie. I've talked to Richard, although I must admit, I thought his story was far-fetched. A lion came from the sky and dropped you on the lawn?"

Her stomach felt queasy, and she grabbed a ginger ale out of the refrigerator in the mudroom and let the cool bubbly stream down her throat. Then she leaned into the wall, not wanting to go back into the kitchen and face the scrutiny of her father.

The whistling teapot broke the tension, and she trudged back to clear the air. "I had a nightmare, Daddy. That's all."

"I believe Richard is under a lot of stress with Parker being ill. He believes your nightmarish dreams are true. If you would see your psychologist more often, all of this silliness will stop." He sighed. "I'll make your breakfast. You look horrible." He frowned. "What's that mark on your neck?"

"A wasp stung me," she lied. "It's nothing."

It was when they were having tea and toast that he hit her with the news that he wanted her to go to Thomas Shrock's wedding.

He looked at her straight on and said firmly, "We'll go as a family. It will stop the gossip before it goes any further."

"Before what goes any further?"

Daniel raised his brows. "A lot went on while Marguerite and I were away. Thomas Shrock attempted to hang himself. Supposedly, it's about a black book that came from this house. The rumors are alarming. I've never heard of such rubbish. People say that seven witches were trying to fight off a dark prince—and you disappeared with him in a cloud of smoke. I wanted to talk to you last night, but you didn't answer your phone. When I spoke with Richard, he said you were sleeping."

Stephanie choked on the toast. Her father didn't know that she'd been away.

He kissed her on the forehead. "See you at dinner, princess."

Stephanie bristled. She couldn't let it go. Her father was almost at the door when she called to him. "Daddy," she said. "We have to talk."

"Can't this wait?" he asked. "I've slept in a chair in the waiting room at the hospital for three nights, and last night I hardly slept because I was worried about you."

"But this is important," she said. Her voice held a sense of urgency.

"We'll talk later. Have another cup of tea, and go write in your journal or whatever you do when you need to resolve a situation."

"No," Stephanie quipped. "It has to be now."

"Is this about Thomas Shrock?" Daniel asked sharply. "Richard said that he told you that Thomas is marrying Maddie Yoder. It's for the best. It's time you did the same. Marry Richard, and have a child."

Mustering up all the courage she could manage, she said in a tight voice. "Having a child doesn't 'fix' a relationship, Daddy. You should know better than to say such a thing."

Judge stared at her with narrow eyes. "What are you insinuating?"

Stephanie gazed at him hard. "Did you adopt me to atone for your sins? Tell me it isn't true, daddy."

Judge dropped his eyes, speechless, the color draining from his face. It was as if his life had just come around in a circle. And it was Richard who had dragged the skeleton out of the closet. He stood, shoulders slumped, a broken man. It sounded so cheap, frivolous, and horrible.

Stephanie stared at him in disbelief.

"You did! My God, you did! You never wanted me—you adopted me to atone for your sins because you had sex with your Mennonite housekeeper. How could you have done such a thing? And I doubt you ever loved Marguerite. Did you?"

Consumed with guilt, he said, "I loved Marguerite years ago, but we grew apart. It was my fault. I stopped showing her affection. Maybe that's why she left to go back to Charlotte that week. She had every reason to hate me. I cheated on her, and I was sorry afterwards. I was trying to make things right with Marguerite, and Hedy knew about a baby in Europe that a monk fathered. Her mother was an opera singer. That baby was you, honey. Hedy and I went to the monastery and got you. And God, as my witness, I loved you from the moment I laid eyes on you. I swear. I'll always believe that God meant me to be your father."

Stephanie stood in front of him, tears streaming down her cheeks. "Did you care for the housekeeper, Daddy? Did you love her?"

"Yes, I loved Susan," he choked. "But a Mennonite and an Englishman can never be together. It would destroy my reputation."

Stephanie backed away in shock. "Your reputation! What about morals and decency… and love?" She took a stance and pointed her finger at Daniel. "After all you did to destroy my relationship with Thomas… you… you… hypocrite!"

Daniel's face turned ashen. "God forgive me," he said.

Stephanie saw red and ran after him, pulling roughly at his sleeve, forcing his gaze.

"We're going to settle this," she screamed. "You have a son."

"That's a lie," Daniel said, turning on his heel.

"I have a letter to prove it," Stephanie barked. "You *can't* deny it."

"You are lying," Daniel said. He rushed away. The screen door slammed behind him.

Tears streamed down Stephanie's face as she stood at the window and watched her father walk down the path and through the gate with the white wooden fence that divided the two properties. Divided—like her feelings that were running amok—the man she admired more than anyone in the world had done a despicable thing.

The Log Cabin

It was awkward going to see Sawyer, but Stephanie was determined to make things right. She had a brother, and he was legally an heir to the family fortune. It was Sawyer whose veins carried her father's blood. Not her. She was adopted—the daughter of a monk. It wasn't about the money. It was about skeletons in the closet that had been hidden away for too long. Hedy had always told her that the sins of the fathers would carry on from generation to generation if not set right.

Sawyer was felling trees near her old cabin, and she could hear the ax hitting its mark—the sound echoing through the valley as she drove her SUV along the cow path.

Anger had made her pick up the phone and call Thomas this morning. He had sounded pained, but she couldn't muster up sympathy to make him feel better. It was over, and they both knew it. She'd been curt and precise.

"I hope you'll be happy," she said. "Now I need to talk to Sawyer."

"He's at the old cabin on your land, felling trees. Maybe Daniel didn't tell you. I take care of the property for Daniel."

"I need to pay you," Stephanie said. "I also owe you for boarding Thunder. Send me an invoice."

"You don't owe me anything. I want to do it."

"This is business, Thomas. I pay my way."

"Don't treat me like this, Stephanie. You don't know what happened."

"I think I do," she said.

"I need to talk to you, Stephanie," he said with a firm voice. "Rumors are circulating that are not true."

Stephanie slammed down the phone.

When Stephanie arrived at the cabin, it was neat and clean. It puzzled her when she put a bottle of water in the refrigerator and found what looked to be a rabbit, cut up and marinating in brine, along with a six-pack of beer. She guessed it was Sawyer's.

She found some sassafras herbs in the cupboard and made a cup of tea. The first taste was bitter, but she swallowed it. Then she trudged out to the side of the house and waved, trying to get Sawyer's attention.

Sawyer saw her and waved back. She gestured for him to come to the house.

Stephanie thought, his look uncertain as he neared.

"I hope you don't mind—Emily permitted me to stay here while I'm felling trees. She said no one has stayed here since your grandmother died."

"Stay as long as you like," Stephanie said with a smile. "Thomas told me you were here. We need to talk."

"I'm starved. Can we do it over dinner? I'm frying up a rabbit for dinner."

"Sure, what can I do?"

"Maybe you could cook the rabbit while I shower," Sawyer said. "I've been felling trees since five a.m."

Stephanie quickly floured the rabbit, then browned it in a cast-iron skillet. She went outside and picked wild flowers. After arranging the bouquet in a white pitcher, she lit a candle. Then went down to the cellar and found a bottle of red wine.

"Smells mighty homey," Sawyer said as he strode into the kitchen, his dark hair wet, smelling fresh of Ivory soap.

"Setting the mood," Stephanie said.

"For what?" Sawyer asked, raising his brows.

"It's just what girls do when they're about to have dinner with someone special," she said, feeling a flutter of anxiety creeping in. He was too good-looking, standing there all fresh, his muscles bulging through his t-shirt. She was staring. She dropped her eyes, reminding herself she was back with Richard. *What was she thinking?*

"It's nothing fancy," Sawyer said, going to the stove and turning the rabbit with a fork.

Stephanie swirled her glass of wine. "My grandmother used to fix it."

Sawyer popped a beer and took a swig. "You're not making a move on me, are you? I saw you last night with Richard on the lawn.". "How much did you see?"

"I saw it all. I was behind the oak tree. The lion dropped you not more than a foot from me. I couldn't believe my eyes. The sorceress told me that a witch from another kingdom said that you'd be coming back on a lion's back. I didn't believe her until I saw it for myself."

Stephanie's heart was thundering. The lion had dropped her next to Sawyer—not Richard. Richard had been in the house. Did she dare tell him?

"Why are you here?" Sawyer asked. "If it's about the letter—I want you to burn it. I don't want your father to know that I'm his son. It's water over the dam."

They heard a noise, a shuffling sound, and when she looked up, her father stood at the doorway.

Stephanie tried to regain her composure as Daniel pulled out a worn wooden chair and sat down next to Sawyer. "Looks cozy," he said, his dark eyes hard. "Flowers, wine. Would you like to explain what you're doing here with an accused murderer?"

"I'm sorry, sir. I'll be going," Sawyer said as he hung his head and stood up. "I was felling trees for Thomas Shrock, and Emily told me I could stay here for a few days while I'm working."

Daniel nodded, "Sit down," he ordered. "I overheard something that I don't understand. What's this about a letter, and you being Stephanie's brother? Are you an impostor?"

"I should go," Sawyer said. "It was nothing."

Stephanie could no longer hold back. She went to her purse, pulled out the letter, and handed it to her father. "This will explain everything."

Daniel was pensive when he read the letter; his face grew stark white. "My God," he said in a choked voice. "How could this be?" He shook his head and stared hard at Sawyer. "I didn't know about you. Believe me."

"It's okay," Sawyer said. "My mother saved the money you gave her, but my grandmother had to use some of it to pay my fine when I was in jail. I have it. You can have it back."

"No," Daniel said, filled with emotion, color returning to his face. "I'm so sorry, son. I'm afraid I let everyone down."

He put his elbows on the table and put his head in his hands. "I know what you're going to think; Susan was a Mennonite. It makes me look like a bigot. Susan has haunted me since it happened. She didn't leave because of the cultural differences—she left because I was married. We both knew she couldn't stay. Marguerite was in Charleston because we weren't getting along." He glanced at Stephanie. "Do you think badly of me?"

"I'm over the shock," she said.

Although some color had returned to his face, he was visibly upset and looked frail; it was hard for her to see him in that state. She'd always held him on a pedestal, and it was difficult watching her *too-perfect* father, whose sins had come back to haunt him, suffer.

"How long have you two known each other?" Daniel asked, his dark eyes darting back and forth between the two of them with hints of suspicion.

"A few weeks," Stephanie said, aware of how it must look to him. She was eager to ease his mind. "I met Sawyer the night of the exorcism at Thomas Shrock's. He saved my life."

Daniel gazed at Sawyer. "I'm grateful. And I'm going to make everything up to you, son. We've lost a lot of time. We'll never get those years back, but I'm going to do the right thing by you. I need to figure out where to start. Do you need anything, son? Money?"

"No, I own a horse ranch," he replied. "You're not obligated to me. We can pretend like this never happened. I didn't want you to know, but Stephanie took the letter. I found it hidden in my grandmother's quilt." Sawyer stopped talking, afraid he was incriminating himself. He also feared that he would get Stephanie in trouble.

The thin line between Daniel's brow and his down turned mouth told Stephanie that Daniel was still in a bit of shock. She worried he might need medication for his heart.

"I have to go," he said. "But tomorrow the wheels are going to turn. You're going to get what's yours, Sawyer. I'm bringing you into the family. I'm going to tell Marguerite."

His eyes scanned Sawyer as if he were seeing him for the first time. "You look just like me. You even have a dimple in your chin. My father and my grandfather had it, too. I could never deny you. I don't know why I didn't see it when you were before me at the courthouse." He paused. "We'll go shopping for clothes, get you a haircut."

Stephanie watched as Sawyer's expression turned from cowed to fearful. She wondered if her father's words had stung his pride. She caught the faint tone of anxiety in his voice when he said, "Sir, I'm a Mennonite. It's too late to change me. I can never be English."

"I understand," Daniel said. "We'll buy Mennonite clothes. But I hope you'll agree to a haircut."

Stephanie felt immense relief when Daniel rose to leave. Sawyer could not avoid the big hug and kiss on the cheek that Daniel gave him before he left. They waved to Daniel from the porch as he drove away, and he waved back.

They ate the rabbit, both in shock about what had just happened. Things were different now. Their lives would never be the same. Sawyer was Daniel's natural son, his rightful heir, and she was adopted, the natural daughter of a monk and an opera singer.

It was dusk, and darkness was approaching. "Let's take a walk down by the creek. Get some air," Sawyer said. They walked alongside each other. There was a faint scent of honeysuckle in the air, and it was cooling off.

"How do you feel?" Her brows furrowed in worry that Daniel might have intimidated him.

He turned toward Stephanie and put his arms around her, his lips brushing her forehead. His arms tightened around her. "I still have feelings for you. And they are not brotherly." He took her hand and led her to a mossy rock by the creek. They sat down, and Sawyer took her hand. "I love you."

"Things are different now," Stephanie said. "You'll be part of the family. I'm sure my father would not have left us alone if he thought we were attracted to each other. You're his son. And even if I am adopted, you're my brother. It wouldn't be right. We have to think of each other differently."

"I don't think I can." He drew her close and kissed her. It was a tender kiss, but not at all brotherly.

Stephanie's heart pounded. "We can't act on our feelings. Let's go back to the house and talk."

The moon was above the trees, and she could see the glow of the candles through the windows as they walked hand in hand back to the house.

They talked all night—until the light of dawn seeped into the bedroom. "I have to go," she murmured. "Daddy knows I've been gone all night. He calls me every night. I'll tell him we had a lot to talk about."

"Well, we did have a lot to talk about."

Stephanie's expression was intense. "I didn't expect it to turn out like this. Do you think we'll ever find a balance? I am your adopted sister, and you are the Judge's natural son—a Stratford."

He embraced her. "I'm still Sawyer Rhodes, a Mennonite. No one will ever take my name away from me. I like who I am. I would never take away my years with my grandmother and my mother, and pretend like they never existed."

"You are my father's son, Sawyer, and nothing can ever change that. Everything has changed for me—I am the daughter of a monk, and my mother was an opera singer who obviously didn't want me, and somehow I will have to accept it."

Sawyer gathered her in his arms. "Tell me this. Do you care for me? Because that's all that matters."

"God help me," Stephanie whispered. "I do love you, Sawyer."

"We'll be discreet," he said, burying his face in her neck. "Your father will never know."

"It's too late," Stephanie said, tearing up. "I have to marry Richard; there are things you don't know." She dashed out the door, feeling betrayed by

Lillian. Her heart told her she loved Sawyer. The Lion had dropped her in the wrong place.

A Rooster Crowed Twice

A rooster crowed twice. Stephanie roused from a dreamless sleep and stretched. Drowsy, she listened for the rooster to crow again, but it didn't. A rooster always crowed three times. It was bad luck if they didn't. She stiffened. Her eyes widened. It wasn't an ordinary day—at four o'clock this afternoon, she would marry Richard and would never be free to live as she saw fit again—a daunting life sentence would be imposed with two simple words "I do."

She had a severe case of wedding jitters and tried to shake them. After breakfast, holding a mug of green tea, she went to the window in the drawing room and looked out. High on the hill at Stratford Place, she observed a swirl of activity: tents that looked like huge marshmallows filled the manicured lawn. White trucks full of flowers were lined up to be unloaded by the wedding planner's assistants. Enormous bouquets of Southern peach roses mixed with trumpet-shaped white Calla lilies, and tiny bell Lilies of the Valley with a touch of greenery would be set on banquet tables, gazebo, and in the main parts of the house.

Oddly, Stephanie felt detached—unable to rid herself of the idea that something would prevent the wedding from taking place. Jitters or a premonition? She sighed and told herself that every bride has felt like this.

She went to the closet, took out her wedding veil, put it on her head, and adjusted it in the mirror. The reflection showed her what she needed to see:

she looked better than she felt. Her nerves weren't showing.

"Mrs. Cooper," she said aloud as she gazed into the mirror, trying to decide if she liked the sound of the name that would soon be hers.

A familiar voice behind her said, "How can you be Mrs. Cooper when you're already Mrs. Shrock?"

"Becca!" Stephanie squealed. "You scared me."

Becca crossed her arms. "It's unlucky to try on your wedding veil before your wedding," she said.

Stephanie adjusted the veil. "That's an old wives' tale. Do you like my veil?"

Becca rolled her eyes. "I like plain and simple. You used to like it, too. I don't know what happened. But I know one thing — a woman cannot marry two men."

Stephanie frowned. "Becca, are you trying to spoil my wedding day?" she scolded. "My marriage to Thomas wasn't legal. I'm sure my father has taken care of it."

There was a loud knock on the door. Stephanie started.

Becca looked out the window. "It's the sheriff."

Stephanie ran down the stairs with Brooks at her heels. She threw open the door. The sheriff and his deputy stood on the doorstep. "They're parking the cars in the field across from Stratford Place," she said, gesturing at Stratford Place.

"That's not why we're here, Steph," the deputy said.

"Come in," Stephanie said, forgetting that she was wearing her nightgown and her wedding veil.

The deputy held out the document, his hands trembling. She had always made him nervous, even in grade school. "Is this your signature?"

Stephanie shrugged. "Yes, it is, Robby. It's nothing."

"It's Robert. I'm a deputy now," he corrected.

"If this is your signature," the sheriff said with a stern voice, "you're married to Thomas Shrock. This is a legal document, and there were witnesses." He was a short, stout man; his belt buckled below his enormous stomach. His broad-brim felt hat sat atop his round baby face, making him appear taller, and he had a speech impediment. It took him forever to get his words out because he was nervous. He'd been tearing up Stephanie's speeding tickets for years so that Daniel wouldn't know. But this was a serious matter not to be ignored.

"That's impossible," Stephanie protested. "It wasn't an actual ceremony; the woman was a sorceress. She isn't a real minister."

"So, it was like…hocus pocus…you're married?" the sheriff asked.

"Sort of…," Stephanie said, turning bright pink. "It didn't take over two minutes."

"The woman who married you is Cynthia Crenshaw," the sheriff said. "She graduated cum laude from Berkley, and has several degrees—one is in Theology. She's a minister, the clerk at the courthouse filed the marriage license, and you are married to Thomas Shrock."

"Does my father know?" Stephanie stammered.

"Yes. He's trying to get the marriage annulled."

Daniel had been silent when he came in the back door. He had heard everything. "I told you not to bother Stephanie about this," he said with a sharp voice.

"She has to know," the sheriff said forthright, "bigamy is a serious offense. It's a crime punishable by six months in jail. I don't want to do it, Stephanie, but if you go through with the wedding, I'll have to take you to jail."

Daniel crossed his arms. "We have five hundred people coming for a wedding, and Marguerite and Marsha are damned well going to give them a wedding. I don't have time to go through the loopholes to annul your marriage to Thomas. We're going through with the wedding. It won't be legal without the license. Later, we'll have a small private ceremony and make it legal. It's a mere technicality: a piece of paper."

Daniel, a history buff, said, "Andrew Jackson married Rachael Donelson in 1790 when she was married to another man. And if the seventh President of the United States can do it, we sure as hell can do it. Her husband knew of their affair and petitioned for a divorce. After they were married, they discovered Rachael's divorce had never been finalized. After her husband divorced her, Rachael and Andrew Jackson had another wedding ceremony.

We will do the same thing. Stephanie will have two weddings."

Her father's urgent haste to have her marry Richard did not sit well with Stephanie. A marriage that was not valid made little sense. "Would you have me do that, Daddy? I doubt the priest would perform the ceremony if he knew I was already married."

"Marguerite's given thousands to the church," Daniel said. "The priest will do whatever she tells him to do. He's her puppet."

Stephanie pulled on her wedding veil. "I don't want to go to jail, Daddy…"

"It was a formality. No one is going to put the daughter of Daniel Stratford in jail. They don't want to lose their job. Besides, five hundred guests from all over the United States have come to Brier Hill County for a wedding: The hotels in this area are all full; we're shuttling people from Columbus from three hotels; the chefs began food preparation yesterday; the wooden dance floor is in the tent—and the orchestra is rehearsing; Three six-tier wedding cakes are sitting in the dining room. Three magazines are sending photographers. We are going through with the ceremony."

Stephanie felt light-headed. She'd never felt so much pressure. "I'll do it, Daddy, if that's what you want." She paused and said, "Does Richard know Thomas won't give me an annulment?"

"Yes, he knows, and he agrees with me. We have to move forward. We can't let Thomas interfere with the wedding."

She fought the feeling of wanting to run away from it all, but remained calm. "Maybe I should go up to the house and speak to Richard about this."

"It's bad luck to talk to the groom the day of the wedding. Richard is with Bradley. They're having lunch and a drink with the wedding planner—going over the wedding details."

"I just want to talk to him for a minute," Stephanie pressed. "This is a legal matter. I'm married to Thomas, and I don't want to get arrested."

"You can't go up there and stir things up," Daniel said. "Marsha and Marguerite are working hard to make this a memorable wedding for you." He paused, taking a long breath. "You and Richard fight like cats and dogs, and we don't need conflict right before the wedding. Everyone has been walking on eggs—every time Richard's cell phone rings, we all freeze. Come hell or high water, you are going to be married at four o'clock today. The horse-drawn carriage will arrive at three forty-five. When you walk out that door, the photographers will start the photo shoot. For once in your life—cooperate."

Stephanie dropped her eyes. "I didn't realize that I was so much trouble to everyone."

After everyone left, Stephanie slumped down in a chair. She was deep in thought when Becca set a cup of tea down on the end table.

"What am I going to do, Becca?" Stephanie asked, hoping Becca wouldn't say something like, 'The sun will come out tomorrow.'

"Call Thomas," Becca said. "Maybe he'll sign the papers."

"He'd be stupid not to sign the papers," Stephanie huffed. "Maddie Yoder is pregnant."

Becca's mouth gaped. "Young Thomas would not do such a thing. He's a deacon."

"It's true. Richard told me we're invited to their wedding."

"He has it all wrong. Maddie is marrying Eli Hershberger. He's the father of her child. Thomas is officiating at the wedding, along with Bishop Jon. Thomas is marrying them—not marrying her."

Stephanie's hand went to her heart. "All this time, I thought Thomas was marrying Maddie."

"Why would he marry Maddie?" Becca asked. "Thomas is married to you."

Stephanie put her hand on her forehead. "That's quite enough, Becca," she said, trying to regain her composure, pleased that Thomas was not getting married.

"Your tea's getting cold," Becca said. "And take that silly veil off your head?"

Stephanie jerked the veil off, tossing it over her head. Then she picked up the phone. "If you don't mind, Becca, I'd like some privacy. I'm calling Thomas."

Becca grinned and dashed out of the room.

Stephanie dialed the number, her face apprehensive. "Thomas, do you have a minute? There's a problem. Could you stop by the courthouse and sign the annulment papers? It seems we're still married."

"That's true," Thomas said. "You can't get a marriage license."

"Don't joke about it. I need you to sign the papers."

"I don't want an annulment. An Amish man marries for life."

Stephanie's green eyes flashed. "Listen to me, the sheriff was here, and I'm going to get into a lot of trouble if you don't sign the papers."

"The scuttlebutt is that Daniel is pressuring you into marrying Richard."

"Is it now?" Stephanie said, her voice high.

"When are you going to stand on your own two feet and stop letting Daniel make your decisions? A girl should be able to choose her husband."

"Richard would make a fine husband for any girl," Stephanie lashed out.

"Maybe he will, but not you. You're already married to me, and I'm not budging."

"Why can't you be reasonable?"

"I am being reasonable. Things are going on behind your back, and I can't let you marry Richard Cooper."

"What is it? Why are you being so secretive?"

"If I tell you the truth, you'll think it's a ploy for me to get you back. It doesn't matter — mother said the rooster crowed twice this morning. It's a bad omen. A rooster always crows three times. I don't think there's going to be a wedding."

"That's superstition," Stephanie said.

Thomas made a chittering sound that sounded like a muskrat.

"Muskrat love," Stephanie said, agitated, remembering the day they'd been out walking by the pond and watched two muskrats building a home with sticks at the pond, and he'd told her that muskrats mate for life.

She had once loved the chittering sound, but now it didn't sit right with her. Everything about the conversation was driving her a little insane…the rooster crowed twice—the incessant chittering.

"For God's sake, Thomas," Stephanie said in a sharp voice. "Stop that chittering. I'm not a muskrat, and I don't care how many times the rooster crows. I'm not the girl you once knew—I'm not fifteen. I've grown up."

There was a click.

Stephanie put her head down on the kitchen table and sobbed. Her words had been brutal, but true. He was a deacon. His people meant everything to him. But the Amish hated her, and she had a scar on her arm to prove it. It had to end with Thomas.

Stephanie trudged up to her bedroom and looked in the mirror, not liking the girl that she saw. Her eyes were red from crying, and she had vast circles under her eyes. She threw herself on the bed, sobbing. *This should be the happiest day of my life, and it isn't. My entire life has been a lie. I'm not Judge Daniel Stratford's daughter. I'm the daughter of a monk who delves in the dark. Why was I born?*

She started when she heard a soft voice that sounded like her grandmother: *You are the girl with the golden ribbon with a golden thread that goes all the way to the heavens. Never be ashamed of who you are. Your birth has already changed many lives.*

Stephanie lay trembling. She was sure it was her grandmother and was too frightened to say a word. She calmed down and went to the mirror. The girl who looked back appeared much wiser.

"I am the girl with the golden ribbon," she whispered. "A ribbon that goes all the way to the heavens. And I am not ashamed that my father is a monk who delves in the dark, or that my mother is an opera singer who abandoned me. And I don't know why this is happening to me, but there is something greater. Something I do not understand."

She smiled at the girl in the mirror. "I can do this," she said with a sigh. Then she turned on her heel and went running down the stairs to find Becca.

"Becca, Becca," she cried out. "We only have an hour. Could you help me with my hair? And you're sitting in the front row so that I can see you. I need you there, Becca. You're the best friend a girl ever had."

"I look a sight," Becca protested. "I'll sit in the back with Emily and the rest of the help."

"You're beautiful just the way you are, but you must put a ribbon in your hair. Please sit in the front row with my parents. It's a wedding, Becca. And you must dance tonight. Maybe you'll meet someone."

Becca looked dubious. "Sometimes you almost make me believe that I'm worthy. You make me feel like I'm somebody. My life would be empty and lonely without you."

"Stop it, Becca. You're going to make me cry."

"It's true. You make everyone's life better. Hedy always said you were a godsend to her. The two of you raised a substantial amount of money for charities. You're only twenty years old and you've done more in your young life than most people do in a lifetime."

"We still need a new school. I'm going to talk to Richard about it. Somehow, we have to raise money for the school."

They went into the craft room, and Stephanie pulled a long pink ribbon from the spool. "No more black ribbons, Becca. Today, you will wear pink to match my flowers." Stephanie cut the ribbon and tied a bow in Becca's hair.

Becca beamed.

The Wedding

June's warmth bathed Stratford Place in golden light as the county's elite clutched their gilt-edged invitations at the iron gates. Whispers had circulated for weeks—would the notorious Stephanie go through with it? The old estate perched on its hill, surrounded by manicured gardens where photographers jostled for position, some scaling trees for the perfect angle. A hush fell over the seated guests as the clip-clop of hoofbeats echoed on the cobblestone.

Through the gates she came, two white stallions drawing her carriage. Her white silk organdy gown caught the light, her blush-rose cascade trembling in her hands. Beneath her long veil, she offered photographers a glowing, practiced smile that revealed nothing of whether the rumors of a runaway bride held any truth, as the horses cantered up the hill toward whatever fate awaited.

The carriage approached, and Stephanie's breath caught at the sea of faces turning toward her. Only when the white gazebo came into view did her racing pulse steady—there stood Richard in his impeccable tuxedo, more striking than any man she'd ever laid eyes on. He stretched his neck, searching for her through the crowd, his face alight with anticipation. In moments, she would take his name as her own.

The carriage halted. Sawyer stood waiting, and Stephanie faltered. Heat rushed to her cheeks, the delicate veil her only shield. He stood shoulder to

The Wedding

shoulder with Daniel, their matching profiles announcing their blood tie to anyone with eyes to see. With a painful courtesy, Sawyer extended his hand, helping her down from the carriage. Their eyes locked.

His lips grazed the delicate barrier of her veil. "This is too difficult," he murmured, his voice breaking, dark eyes betraying everything words couldn't say.

A V-formation of geese cut across the sky, their honking drawing all eyes upward. The bride and the handsome Mennonite beside her tilted their faces to the heavens in perfect synchronicity, the moment's tension dissolving. Cameras clicked, capturing the tableau: wild birds against azure, the bride's wonder-struck expression, her fingers digging into his shoulder. Bridal magazines would devour such serendipity.

While everyone tracked the geese, none witnessed the raven's descent—black wings against blue—as it released a dark ribbon onto the rose-strewn crimson carpet just as Sawyer lowered her to stand.

Five hundred pairs of eyes. Five hundred waiting breaths. Stephanie hadn't imagined the weight of such collective attention. Daniel's arm became her anchor as she forced herself to face the crowd.

"Smile, Stephanie," called a photographer, his flash blinding her.

She forced a smile, thankful for the veil concealing tears that transformed the audience into watercolor smudges. Her white linen shoes found the black ribbon. Something cold slithered through her veins. Her pulse hammered against her throat. She leaned into her father, seeking stability in his frame.

Only a few steps separated Stephanie from Richard, yet she kept her gaze fixed on the red carpet beneath her satin heels. Her heart fluttered against her ribs like a trapped bird while her mind screamed: run. At the altar stood the man everyone envied her for—tall with a cleft chin, movie-star handsome, his adoring smile radiating an adoration she couldn't face.

A bumblebee darted into her path, circling her veil with a persistent buzzing. Stephanie's muscles tightened, but she pressed forward. Disappointing her father would sting far worse than any insect. Then came Raven, swooping across her vision, breaking her careful rhythm. She stumbled, losing step with her father's measured pace.

Squaring her shoulders, Stephanie tracked the bee's erratic dance while Raven settled atop the rose-draped gazebo, a dark sentinel among pink and white blossoms.

Richard's smile faltered. He dabbed at perspiration beading his forehead with a monogrammed handkerchief. The possibility that she might flee had crossed his mind, especially now with her visible distress. Yet his love remained unwavering, his ice-blue eyes pleading her forward.

From its perch, Raven watched, its obsidian gaze piercing through her like a prophecy.

Daniel clasped Richard's hand at the altar, satisfaction clear in his firm grip. The Stratford dynasty had found its match—his best friend's son possessed the requisite wealth, ambition, and pedigree. Daniel's lips brushed Stephanie's forehead before he strode to join Marguerite, claiming her hand as he'd just relinquished his daughter's.

Beside Richard, Stephanie knelt, doubt fluttering in her chest. The priest's face glistened with perspiration beneath his vestments. His golden crucifix held her gaze until she averted her eyes, feeling dizzy.

A buzzing approached. The bee alighted where Damien's teeth had once broken her skin—searing pain. The world tilted, darkened.

Damien's vengeance found her.

Color drained from Stephanie's face as she fought for breath.

"Anaphylactic shock," Richard shouted. "EpiPen—anyone?"

"Here!" Marguerite's friend called out, rushing forward.

Bradley delivered the pen to Richard, who plunged it into Stephanie's thigh.

Mopping his brow with a handkerchief, Richard squeezed her hand.

Though present, Stephanie tumbled through the darkness that blazed to the Crimson Room, captured in Damien's embrace, his tormented face mere inches from hers.

She returned Richard's squeeze, conscious of her surrounding family: Daniel, Marguerite, Parker, Marsha, Richard, and Sawyer.

"The mortal will never have you," Damien's voice cut through the air like a blade. "You are mine alone."

The Wedding

Caught between realms and fighting for survival, she countered, "You relinquished your claim when you traded me away. The curse has been broken."

"I did not give you up," he thundered.

"Your lies cannot bind me. I refuse to serve a prince of darkness for eternity."

"Your fate is to be my bride. I remain your Lord."

"No longer," she whispered. "I embrace The Light."

Those simple words coursed through her veins like liquid courage.

In an instant, radiance surrounded her as King Midas materialized before them.

"Release her," Midas ordered. "Our bargain is complete. She belongs to me now."

Damien's grip loosened. As he dissolved into shadow, Stephanie glimpsed humble women in prayer, kneeling in devotion. A revelation struck her—countless others battled darkness not with steel but with faith.

She saw Joseph praying, and he was a handsome man; they had restored his face. And she knew the last seal was broken, and she was free to love.

Stephanie hurtled through cosmic planes until she beheld it—a celestial palace crafted from precious gems: ruby, diamond, jade, and opal, glittering beyond imagination. The Jewel Box? Understanding dawned. King Midas had claimed her, just as Lillian had foretold. She yearned to remain, but a commanding voice resonated: Your journey continues, child; Earth awaits your return.

She clung to the fading vision—I must find my way back to the Jewel Box—as she sped up through the infinite expanse. A peculiar figure appeared—a Mad Hatter with an emerald top hat and an inverted umbrella of matching hue.

"Please help me," she implored. "I need to return to the Jewel Box."

"I'm afraid you're headed in quite the wrong direction," he replied with a wide, toothy smile.

Stephanie crashed to the floor. Her eyes fluttered open—her body weak, but her mind sharper than ever before. Had she escaped? Dread crawled through her veins. Damien's presence still lingered, phantom fingers around her throat.

The cross swung like a pendulum before her eyes. The priest knelt beside her, his thumb tracing oil across her forehead. Last Rites? Something fierce ignited within her—a refusal to surrender. With newfound strength, Stephanie's lips curled into the slightest smile as she snatched the cross from the priest's neck. Triumph surged through her as she pressed the metal to her lips, eyes closing as she felt its power pulse against her skin.

"She lives," the priest whispered, clutching the empty gold chain. His eyes darted to Richard, questioning.

"Continue the ceremony," Richard commanded, tension threading his words.

"I will not," Stephanie breathed. "I've stood at death's threshold." Her gaze locked with the priest's. "You prepared me for death, yet I chose life. Whatever moments remain are mine alone—not my father's, not anyone's—mine."

"What's happened to you?" Richard demanded.

"I met a Mad Hatter at the crossroads," she said.

"Dear God," Richard whispered.

The Celebration

Marguerite stood, shoulders squared, and addressed the bewildered guests. "A severe allergic reaction to a bee sting has prevented the ceremony today. Though there will be no wedding, we hope you'll stay and celebrate with us, regardless."

Hours passed in a blur of champagne that flowed like water and music that echoed throughout the hills and valleys. Stephanie watched couples twirl around the dance floor, Richard among them. He had barely looked her way since the announcement. She rested her head against her father's shoulder, gathering courage.

"Daddy," she whispered, "can you forgive what happened? When that bee stung me, something took hold. I fought it with everything—prayers, will, even the blessed oil from Father Thomas."

Daniel's arm tightened around her shoulders. "We're just grateful you're still here with us," he murmured. "You gave us quite a fright."

Across the ballroom, Richard's laughter rose above the music as he regaled his fraternity brothers with stories. "He hasn't spared me a glance all evening, but he's danced with every woman here except me," Stephanie sniffed.

Sawyer, sitting beside her, leaned closer. "I've been watching you all evening. May I have this dance?"

The corners of Stephanie's mouth lifted. "I'd like that."

On the dance floor, Sawyer was a smooth dancer, his hand warm against the small of her back. She rested her cheek against his shoulder, breathing in his familiar scent. "That bee sting was almost a blessing," she murmured. "It stopped everything before it was too late."

"I've been hoping for a miracle," Sawyer's voice was low in her ear. "You know my feelings haven't changed."

Stephanie looked up at him. "Mine haven't either… but timing is everything."

"Maybe our timing is now," he said. "What's standing in our way?"

"I have plans—my grandmother's legacy. The school for the village children, the medical clinic."

"Those can be our plans," Sawyer said. "I want to build them with you."

"Let's not wait," she whispered. "Cake and champagne now, the cabin tonight."

"You're certain?" His brow furrowed. "Your father—"

"I'm sure. Sometimes it takes a bee sting and a Mad Hatter to remind you how fleeting life is." She squeezed his hand. "I want you beside me for whatever comes next. Marriage can wait—I have college to finish, places to see. But if you're patient, I'll wear your ring someday."

Sawyer's eyes lit with a warmth she'd never seen before. "Before you, I never imagined settling down," he admitted, spinning her in a slow circle across the floor.

Later, they quietly slipped away with boxes of food, cake, and champagne, heading to Sawyer's cabin. Flames flickered in the fire pit as they sat on a weathered log, watching fireflies dance like stars close to the ground. When a falling star streaked across the sky, they fell silent in awe.

To Stephanie, that golden streak carried whispers from another realm. Someday, she thought, she would reunite with them all—Lillian, Nettles, the Sorceress, and the Seven Witches who had illuminated her darkest hours.

"Look," she breathed, eyes fixed on the star-studded sky. "I could swear

The Celebration

that's the Sorceress and her Witches soaring by on broomsticks." She laughed. "Maybe I am living a fairy tale life after all."

She couldn't know the truth those words contained.

In distant realms, Joseph's blue eyes shimmered as he gazed upon her. "My daughter," came his whisper. Pride filled his chest. He would never be ashamed to show himself to her again. Lucifer had restored his face, and he was once again a handsome man.

Joseph's love traversed the divide, and Stephanie's heart suddenly felt whole—she was the 'girl with the golden ribbon,' tethered to celestial heights by a golden thread unbreakable.

Owl hooted from a branch overhead, drawing her smile upward.

"Are you happy?" Sawyer's voice was tender, his eyes searching hers.

"Completely," she answered, her face luminous. "I always knew you'd come—my prince."

When their lips met, it was a promise without end.

A kiss of forever.

The end.

About the Author

Meg Anne Brighton lives near Charm, Ohio. Other riveting novels include: The Silence of the Loons, The Nephew's Proposition, and Susan's Mirror Image. The second book in the Brier Hill series is underway: The Sorceress and the Seven Witches.

Also by Meg Anne Brighton

Silence of the Loons
HISTORICAL FICTION. BASED ON A TRUE STORY.

In the heart of Maury County, Tennessee, during the tumultuous 1920s, the rugged hills echo with the eerie cries of cougars at night, and shadowy figures of moonshiners clandestinely brew their potent "white lightning." Life is about surviving any way you can.

Fourteen-year-old Pricilla Powell wants more out of life and flees an arranged marriage set up by her matchmaker mother to her moonshiner, gunslinger cousin.

Driven by desperation, Pricilla makes a daring escape and finds refuge in Belle Barker's saloon as a kitchen helper. Through cracks in the kitchen door, and the scent of whiskey mingled with sweat and tobacco, Pricilla learns about life. Belle and the girls at the speakeasy stir a spirit of rebellion in her. Realizing her innocence and desire for more out of life, Belle devises a clever ruse to stage Pricilla's death, granting her the chance to flee to Nashville with a mysterious benefactor.

The beautiful debutante is happy until fate intervenes; a trial summons her back to her hometown, where she must confront the chilling reality of facing the man who embodies her greatest fears. The stakes are high, and the battle for her freedom is just beginning.

SUSPENSE, MYSTERY, ROMANCE, MURDER

Susan's Mirror Image
PSYCHOLOGICAL THRILLER

Susan James, a librarian, flees her violent husband, Blaine, after uncovering evidence that he murdered his first wife. A psychic warns that her life is in danger.

After beginning a new life with an FBI undercover agent, Derrick Hampton, she discovers his deceased wife, Jenny, died mysteriously several months earlier.

Held in the grip of a powerful billionaire and emotionally scarred by Blaine's gaslighting, Susan struggles with deception and betrayal.

Blaine is a ticking time bomb, stalking Susan.

The Nephew's Proposition
A ROMANCE THRILLER

A captivating story about a charismatic billionaire, Charlie Dern, a Gatsby-like figure who convinces his hospice nurse, Anne Jones, to quit her job and help him complete his bucket list.

Charlie's love of danger turns his bucket list into a dangerous challenge, intensified by his old mob ties.

The greatest threat is Gray, Charlie's nephew, who tempts Anne with an alluring offer that sparks romance and adds a fiery edge to this dangerous and thrilling story.

www.ingramcontent.com/pod-product-compliance
Lightning Source LLC
Chambersburg PA
CBHW022101090426
42743CB00008B/682